Alkuajatus

The Original Thought

The Little Manual of Life

*"We are walking in a dream, thinking it's the real.
We are sleeping in the real, thinking it's a dream."*

www.alkuajatus.org

Alkuajatus, The Little Manual of Life

Copyright: Hannu 1987-2011
Author: Hannu
Cover, illustrations and layout: Hannu
Original language: Finnish, ISBN 9789524982900
Original title: Alkuajatus - Elämän pieni käsikirja, published 2010
Translation: Alkuajatus Translation Team - The responsible translator: Sami
1st edition in English, published 2012

Publisher: Books on Demand GmbH, Helsinki, Finland
Manufacturer: Books on Demand GmbH, Norderstedt, Germany

ISBN 978-952-286-530-4

Table of contents

Welcome to the world of Alkuajatus

Alkuajatus is a thought that is created by its author, and which within the boundaries of the existing classifications has to be defined as a religious philosophy.

The name of the thought is Alkuajatus (The Original Thought), since it concerns the fundamental nature, thought and reason of man, which to their origin are spiritual and individual.

The purpose of Alkuajatus is to bring people the keys to the fundamental questions about the inner world and its relation to the outer world, and vice versa.

This book presents the basics of Alkuajatus and they focus on the human life from the viewpoint of one life, which is the first and most important problem when searching for freedom and when conducting the world to be as we originally wanted it to be.

Alkuajatus addresses both the obtaining of inner clarity and the freeing of the life-creating ability, since life can't be detached from the inner reality, which is its origin and which should be what controls life.

For one who honestly seeks, Alkuajatus will give the tools for the search of the truth. One who doesn't seek, or doesn't want to find, won't get anything useful out of Alkuajatus, and it will never open up to him.

I wish all a genuine life and rewarding moments of reading.

Hannu

Preface

Alkuajatus

Alkuajatus is the reflection of inner reality on to this world.

Alkuajatus is a creation that describes the inner original thought, in other words the original inner world, its nature and its relation to this world.

Its only source is the observation of the inner world and the outer world from the viewpoint of the inner world.

Similarities with matters presented in other sources, known or unknown to the writer of Alkuajatus, are a result of the simple fact, that those who observe same areas will at least partly make the same or similar discoveries.

The similarities between the discoveries don't necessarily mean, that they mean exactly the same. The understanding of Alkuajatus requires that each matter is understood in the way Alkuajatus means.

Other thoughts

In the past there have been persons, who have observed their inner reality and told what they have seen there. That which they have told, is told from their viewpoint. If you want to familiarize yourself with them, familiarize yourself with them as entireties, without mixing them with other descriptions of the found.

Only the original description as unchanged is valuable. All compilations, copies and changed descriptions have distorted the original message, and therefore they are more or less valueless. They have been mixed with imagination and thinking. They lead astray. Often they are directly poisonous and have been made to be tools of power.

Only the one who personally has brought up the full knowledge can, on the level he found, tell about it so that the told is genuine.

Those who have had sufficient insights of the original description won't change it. Changes are made only by those, who don't understand it, but want to teach or form it into a tool of power.

The purpose of Alkuajatus

The purpose of Alkuajatus is to help the restoration of the personal religion-function.

Alkuajatus is a tool for the finding of the real self and for the restoration of the original purpose of life.

Alkuajatus is a map, with which one seeks a destination that is ultimately Self.

Alkuajatus is not a religion that tells the purpose of life to the human, or defines good manners and morals from the outside. Alkuajatus guides the human to his real selfhood, where the answers, and more importantly, the understanding of the basics of life already exist. It can't be taught, it must be found through insight, which is equal to finding it from within.

Alkuajatus is not the truth, it is a description of the truth and it guides to find the answers within each and everyone, which is where the truth is. Alkuajatus doesn't offer answers, but guidance that leads to insight.

Alkuajatus can be used as a religion like the present religions, but not as an institution of spiritual power that is binding and controls from above, but within the frames of the law of helping, which is defined by Alkuajatus.

Alkuajatus differs from the existing religions so that it doesn't try to raise the human into the values defined by the community, but it strives to help to bring forth the values that come out of each and everyone himself.

The use of Alkuajatus

So, Alkuajatus is not the truth, but it is a tool that describes that which is true. Therefore the studying of Alkuajatus in the sense, where one wants to learn it to be able to use it as a consequent truth, doesn't lead to the understanding of the truth.

Alkuajatus is like a map, and it mustn't be mistaken for the forest, but it needs to be understood as a tool for finding. The truth can't be put into words, it can't be drawn into pictures, it can only be described.

One can memorize Alkuajatus writings, if one sees it to be the best way for oneself, but for it really to open up, one must find Alkuajatus from within. It is already there, it is only forgotten.

Reading the book won't open up the view instantly. If one wants to benefit from the book in the best possible way, the book should be read many times and in peace and quiet, again and again. Then the book functions as an aid for concentration. What is focused on isn't the book, but what the book describes.

The understanding of the book's contents is made easier if one, when re-reading it, approaches the written as if it was the first time. With this can be avoided, that one only strengthens the own earlier thought-images of the matter.

The knowledge presented by Alkuajatus is a tool. The insight of it, in other words finding it from within, is the goal. Knowledge is used to open the lock, with insight one steps into the room.

While reading the book, one mustn't stare at individual sentences, but has to picture the written as a whole in a context, and link it to Alkuajatus.

Looking at an individual sentence and linking it to something else than what is meant gives the wrong result. One must remember that what is meant here is in these writings, not in the readers mind or any other writings. This way many misunderstandings can be avoided and the understanding of the matter is made easier.

The using of the book as an aid to focus makes the finding of the described easier, since with its help the focus can better be directed on the actual matter. It is easier to move with a map in hand, than in memory. This way many stray paths can be avoided.

The purpose of the pictures in the book is not to be anything else but aids in clarifying each presented thought. Don't use the pictures to observe the matters in ways that aren't based on the text associated with the picture. The pictures aren't necessarily related in any way to other pictures, so don't use them to create a collection of pictures that would be some kind of entirety. Notice, that the truth can't be drawn in pictures.

In the book, the world and oneself is observed from the viewpoint of the inner world, and therefore the writings can't be evaluated by using the world's thought's conception of reality. The world's thought's idea of reality differs strongly from Alkuajatus, and Alkuajatus, or the inner reality, can't be understood from its viewpoint.

Alkuajatus is not a societal opinion for how society should function in different matters. The parts that concern society, as well as the other parts that concern the conventional life, are there to help seeing the world's lie from the viewpoint of the own will's freedom.

Observing the truth is at everyone's own responsibility. If the person doesn't do it himself, nothing will ever be found, and nothing gets better. If Alkuajatus is held interesting, is discussed and thought about, nothing will get clearer. Only the confronting of oneself and the growth of inner honesty produces results. It can't be done by thinking. For that, one has to learn to listen to one's real self.

Alkuajatus viewpoint

The purpose of Alkuajatus is to aid in raising the consciousness of mankind, in other words to aid in the growth of inner honesty. That is its only purpose.

Many matters and reasons are, seen from the inner viewpoint, such that the persons aren't aware of them. In other words the reason for some way to act isn't the result of conscious thinking. In the consciousness there might be an explanation for the reason, but by internally observing, the more original reason can be found. The finding of that more original reason is the prerequisite for solving the problem.

Alkuajatus looks at matters from the viewpoint of the free inner reality. It doesn't try to adapt to the present world and look for answers to it from its viewpoints, but it wants to free people to find themselves more and to create the world, they in accordance to their original will want. Alkuajatus is therefore not societal discussion, it solely and exclusively works for the cause of inner reality.

Alkuajatus doesn't judge anyone, it understands all, but nothing changes the fact that the consciousness of the human must grow, so that the world can change into the place we would want it to be.

While the consciousness grows, the world changes under its own weight. The changes are made by people themselves and as they see fit. Alkuajatus isn't a guide to anything else but the finding of the real selfhood.

To find Alkuajatus

To really find is for some parts faster and for other parts slower. Every person has his own easy and difficult parts. The progress is completely individual, and there is no reason to keep an eye on others and compare one's own progress with theirs.

The only correct point of comparison is the own progress towards the area defined by the own original will and the level of the insights. Everyone has his own, and there is no other goal to strive towards to, if one wants to find what he was supposed to find.

It is not a question of anything such where comparing to others would in any way be useful.

The progress isn't an evenly progressing and easily measurable event. At times is can seem fast and at times it can feel like nothing is happening. Even long and dull periods of time can pass, where the person might mistake to believe that nothing is happening. However, if there is an honest strive and a sufficient focus on the matter, progress will happen, even if it doesn't feel like it.

The progress can best be seen in the long term changes. Even if it would have felt like nothing has happened, the person can at times discover, that even significant changes have occurred.

This phenomenon is caused by that when one is confronting areas that are in the unconsciousness, one is constantly confronting something that isn't necessarily very comfortable. Even if the person is doing progress, he is still confronting unconscious areas, and the feeling it produces might feel very unchangeable.

This could be compared to that one pushes a large object in a wide space, where there are no points of comparison to discover the movement. It might feel like the object isn't moving, even when it is, since the person continues the same performance and its moving is equally difficult all the time, and there is nothing to compare the change of the object's position to.

As a whole the finding of the sought viewpoint requires a lot of time, and one shouldn't be hasty with it. The most significant thing is to see the truth. The truth doesn't reward speed, it rewards the authenticity of the insight.

When one has an insight of something, there is reason to verify many times if the insight was authentic or not. The good feeling of an insight comes from an untrue insight as well as an authentic one, since the good feeling can come out of that one believes to have had an insight.

Therefore there is reason to have a calm attitude towards the matter, and to be ready to question any idea that one has come to.

Something that has been verified many times is more likely to be true on some level, than a sudden insight that is accepted without verification. There is no reason to not to verify it many times and not to constantly be prepared to understand some matter even better.

The truth is not what we wish or believe it to be, and neither does it change to anything else because of several reviews.

The object of observation

At first the object of observation is primarily the inner reality, since only that way the own viewpoint can be moved closer to Self. Observation of the environment is for the most part significant only after that the viewpoint, from which one observes, provides the conditions to understand the environment.

Observation of the environment is primary only in such cases where the person is suppressed by many problems, so that he isn't able to focus on the observation of the inner world.

Then he must first reveal the lies that cause the problem, so that their strength is canceled. Overcoming them requires understanding on the level of a sufficient viewpoint, in which case they are revealed and their strength disappears.

If the overcoming of that kind of problems is too difficult in that specific moment, then one must settle with weakening their strength and putting them aside. In their case one must settle with that they will be solved later.

The cleaner the person can observe the world, while remaining in the viewpoint of his own real person, the better he understands the nature of the world. His possibility to see the world's lie improves while the viewpoint approaches Self.

When the person begins to observe his inner world, and also the outer world, striving to understand them better, he is capable of understanding them on some level. The level rises when the observation is continued, and gradually he approaches the level that is his basic level. The basic level means the level that is the starting level seen from the viewpoint of the fulfilling of his own will.

Only from his starting level can he fully start to fulfill his own will. Before that the search for the starting level is urgent, and it should be a very central matter. Other activities shouldn't then be rushed, and they shouldn't be valued to be more important than the crucial need.

After the reaching of the own starting level, the raising of the level normalizes, and the level is gradually raised in accordance with the need. Then the person is fulfilling his actual purpose and his focus is extroverted. He observes the world with his own eyes and creates his life.

The problem with life is solved so that first one solves the inner problem, which is the lost connection to Self and the own real will. When the person finds his own real will, he knows what he originally wanted to do. After that he can focus on solving the problems considering that doing, which is knowledge and skill and making its performing possible.

From the viewpoint of one who lives an ordinary life, it easily happens so that he considers the life defined by the world's thought as the central thing, and tries to use the observation of the inner reality as a tool for the life defined by the world's thought. The inner reality can't however be subjected into being its tool, since the inner reality is the viewpoint from where the real own will's life is created, and the world as a creation is its tool.

The explaining and presentation of Alkuajatus

A person who is presenting Alkuajatus, presents it from within his own viewpoint. He can't do anything else. His presentation is precisely as far from Alkuajatus as he himself is from it and the complete insight of it.

The same applies to a person who explains it. He is also within the boundaries of his own viewpoint in relation to it.

Presentation is to some extent necessary, since the furthering of Alkuajatus requires presentation of it.

The explaining of Alkuajatus is rarely needed, since the original writings of the thought are available, and they are the surest offered description of what is sought for. Therefore one has to be careful with explaining and use it only when it happens to be necessary.

If the person tends to mostly explain Alkuajatus, or present as his own thoughts altered versions of Alkuajatus, he puts himself as an obstacle between the helped person and Alkuajatus.

Therefore if it in some situation is advantageous for the person's progress to explain something, one must always remember to say, that the explanation doesn't represent the viewpoint of Alkuajatus and that the viewpoint of Alkuajatus can be found in the original writings, and recommend the using of them.

There is a risk that the explanation remains in the ideas of the helped and harms the straight relation to Alkuajatus writings, and slows down the person's progress. Explanations are very exceptionally necessary.

Explaining without doing harm is a person, who is sufficiently progressed in Alkuajatus and his basic level of consciousness is at least the same or exceeds the level of consciousness of the targeted person. The basic level of consciousness is the basic level of the person's own will, in other words the level where his life is meant to be created from.

Misuse of Alkuajatus

Alkuajatus can be misused by starting to use it as a source for thoughts that one uses to develop his own imagined truths by, in his opinion, thinking logically.

Alkuajatus doesn't open up with thinking, and it can't be dealt with by thinking correctly within the frames of the logic of the world's thought. What is achieved that way is not in any case true.

Combining parts of Alkuajatus with other thoughts never produces the correct result. Other thoughts are other thoughts, and Alkuajatus is its own. Their cross-breeding isn't possible. Neither is it done by anyone who understands Alkuajatus, since he would see such as an action that clutters things.

To take individual sentences or presented thoughts from the entirety of Alkuajatus, and dealing with them based on some other thought is to distort Alkuajatus. The purpose of the distortion is not to tell about Alkuajatus, but only how the quotation in the teller's opinion would fit his own ways of thinking, which has nothing to do with Alkuajatus. It is like one would take the steering wheel of a car and publicly have as an opinion, that this steering wheel isn't at all appropriate as a wheel to a bicycle.

Modifications made of Alkuajatus are in one way or another always results of thinking, and a collection of untruths built on an imaginary level. If someone builds such and spreads them to others, it is always a question of lust for power. He is after something that generates money, power and glory, or one of those. He isn't on the cause of the truth. He wants to create an image according to which he has reached something, but he hasn't reached anything that would be true. He tries to imitate knowledge from one or many sources, without really understanding any of them.

Alkuajatus can also be used to, with untrue pretences, understand the activities of people. In those cases the person doesn't understand, and doesn't try to understand Alkuajatus. Instead he might try to invent ways to manipulate people in accordance with his shady goals.

A person who is moderately familiar with Alkuajatus is capable of revealing such lies, and those have no effect on him. Still they might be of harm to people who are already ensnared by the world's lies. The state of the lie in the world will not get much worse, since the lie is always weak in front of the truth, and there is no lie that one who seeks the truth couldn't reveal.

To present oneself as a representative of Alkuajatus is one form of misuse. Then the person tries to be an instructor and a teacher of Alkuajatus. He might imagine that he knows Alkuajatus, for instance after reading this book. With that he seeks money or glory, or both. An honest person doesn't pretend to be an instructor, or an expert, if he really isn't a guide within the meaning of Alkuajatus. To become a guide within the meaning of Alkuajatus doesn't happen fast, and not on one's own.

Here it might be worth noting, that a person who in some occasions presents Alkuajatus isn't guilty of misuse. One can be enthusiastic about the matter, it can be presented and spoken of. Misuse is only to pretend being something one is not, in other words to create untrue images.

Outline

Whose life?

The person acts out of thought. The only life-controlling factor for each and everyone is what thought model he uses for his life. Nothing else controls the life of the person.

The life of the person is owned by the instance, whose thoughts control his life. If those thoughts aren't his own, they belong to someone else, and he doesn't have a life, but is a robot working under external programming. The person's relation to his own life is as a bystander.

The normal condition in the world is that the life of the person is controlled by something else than his own original will. The more aware the person is of this, the greater is the conflict he experiences and the more pain he feels.

The amount of pain is equal to his own experience of the distance between the present state and the wanted state.

The pain can be avoided by growing the consciousness of Self, or by lowering it until it falls into oblivion.

The life is his, who is in the viewpoint of its creating.

What controls my life?

The person experiences to exist and acts based on the thought he has in that moment.

To understand this, one can observe his own experiences, where he has changed his idea of something. When the state before the change is compared to the state after the change, one can make the discovery that the actions changed as a consequence of the change of thought.

The comparing should be performed by focusing enough, and really see that this is true. One should not believe it, nor look at it in a way that makes one understand it. One must look as deep as possible inside him and really see that it is true and very real. Then it is to see, otherwise it is only to think.

This kind of seeing requires peaceful observation of the matter, and it should be observed several times. Each time the observation should last for so long that the seeing, in other words the insight, becomes better than before.

The clearer the person can see the event inside him with his own eyes, the sharper he understands it to be a very real event, and the insight gains strength.

As a result of this observation, one can discover that the only thing that controls the life of each and everyone is the thought model that is being used. The person's life isn't controlled by anything else.

Who creates my thoughts?

Besides what was stated above, one can during the observation discover that it is possible to change the thought, in other words what controls life. When a deep enough understanding is reached, one will notice that it can't be changed by anyone else besides the person himself.

The thought of the person is created by himself and it is changed by himself, and it can't be done by anyone else. The person is the almighty ruler of his own thoughts.

The life controlling effect of the outer forces isn't based on that it controls it, it is based on that it gets the person to control his life in accordance with the desires of an outer instance.

To the extent the person's life is controlled from another than Self's viewpoint, the origin of the thoughts that control the person's life is somewhere else. His life is controlled by someone else, but he himself performs it.

How did I end up to this?

A human copies thoughts from his environment since birth. He observes the humans around him and his senses are much more sensitive at that stage than later on. It is easy for him to see the thoughts of people on a much deeper level, than what people speak of.

He sees behind what the adults speak of, therefore he can copy even such thoughts the adults try to hide. The child copies his environment without criticizing it at all. When he grows older, he starts to some extent choose what he copies.

This copying has its own clear and logical reason. The child has, due to expediency, to build a copy of his environment, for him to reach a viewpoint where he is a part of the environment. The first step when creating life is to take a viewpoint, which is created to the environment where the child is in that moment.

The advantage of the copying is the joining with the environment of life by adopting its viewpoint. Without this joining he would have a great conflict with his environment, which wouldn't be good for his life at its beginning.

The disadvantage is the copied environments distance to Self. The child has to create a distance to himself to reach the starting point of his life. Reaching the starting point of life is a part of life and it has to do with the reasons of life, in other words there is nothing wrong with it as a function.

In the present world, the distance between the persons and Self is so great, that very few can preserve even a weak connection to their real Self. The actual problem is born out of that the distance to Self grows to be so great, that is clouds the consciousness of Self, or might even cut off the connection to Self completely.

Who lives my life?

He lives, whose original thought is fulfilled.

Since a thought that subjects the life of others isn't the real original thought of anyone, we could say that nobody lives, but that we with joined forces maintain a lot of errors.

Since a complete bypassing of Self rarely is fulfilled, we could fine down this claim and say that many live their life to a small extent.

From the individual's viewpoint the first question is that does he live his own life.

Do I want or do I wish?

When the own will is in a passive condition, we can't say that the person wants. If he only thirsts for the fulfilling of his will without acting, he is wishing, not wanting.

Will is fulfilled only when there is action aiming to achieve the fulfilling of the will.

Who experiences life?

He experiences, who is in it.

The person experiences his life himself, regardless of who controls it. All consequences of life fall upon himself, regardless of how or why it ended up where it did.

There are a lot of those who willingly choose the values and the direction of life on behalf of the person, but no matter how it ended up, he will live with the consequences regardless of what happened and why.

The consequences, nor the experience of them, aren't possible to move to someone else. Therefore there is reason to strive towards making one's own decisions, which consequences one has to live with anyhow.

Who is responsible for my life?

We are ourselves in the key position.

We could easily think that the one in control is responsible, but we can't get around the fact, that the executive force is nevertheless each and everyone himself. Even if he is a victim of deception, he still is the executer.

Naturally the deceiver has his responsibility, but if we put our focus in that direction, we will never solve the actual problem, in other words we will not recapture our own life.

Each and everyone is responsible for his own life and his own condition, depending already on the facts that it wasn't created by anyone else, and that it can't be corrected by anyone else but the person himself.

The source of deceit, in other words the deceiving person, is himself in a deceived condition, and most likely he isn't even the original creator of the deceiving thought.

His responsibility is to stop deceiving and to take responsibility for himself, so that he can reach the viewpoint of his own real will, which fundamentally is what he wants, even if he might not be aware of it.

In any case each and everyone is responsible for himself, and there is no other functional way of seeing it, since everyone can only correct himself.

If something in life isn't in a state that is in accordance with the own will, it depends on some problem the person has. The deceivers only use that problem to their advantage. When that problem is solved, one is a winner and in a better condition for the future.

Whose fault?

The actual reasons to the situation of the world lie way back in our history. One could of course trace them, but it wouldn't lead to what is essential, in other words it wouldn't correct this moment.

The persons who take part in the misleading of a child that is born, are mostly deceived themselves and not the origin of the deceit. They are the closest link of a long chain.

The reason to why the person isn't in his own viewpoint is

ultimately that he agreed to be deceived and fulfilled it. Even if he on a practical level hardly had any other choice, he still was the executer.

Other reasons are explanations, even understandable ones, but they were not and are not in a key position, and therefore they are not the actual reason why the life of the person was led astray.

The problem can't be solved if the guilt to the own condition is placed somewhere else, since nothing but a self performed correction of the own life brings the wanted result.

The existence of deceit is a different problem, and it also has to be solved, but it is a secondary problem seen from the viewpoint of the person's life. The primary problem is his own condition. Only to the degree he corrects his own condition is he capable of helping to solve the problem of deceit. The correction of his condition already reduces the force of deceit, since he no longer is a part of it.

The guilty ones to the existence of deceit are from today's viewpoint those who continue it, in other words we're all guilty to some extent. To the extent we manage to stop doing it ourselves, we're also free of guilt.

Who can change?

He can change, who realizes that he can.

Who changes?

He changes, who moves from wishing to will in relation to his own self.

What is life?

We could just as well be in the absolute, in a state of all-connection, aware of everything, as one consciousness, where no one has any distance to anyone.

As a matter of fact we are that even now, since the viewpoint of lowered consciousness is only the maintained way of observing things. We haven't become separated from the all-connection and we aren't even able to become separated from it.

Life is a purposely chosen viewpoint of lowered consciousness that is essential if we want to create an experience of a limited existence. The alternative is the all-connection, in other words the absolute truth.

Behind all life and all material existence is in some way a being, or beings, that belongs in the mentioned all-connection.

The limited existence is, seen from the individual's perspective, a viewpoint for life that each and everyone himself has chosen. Seen from the absolute viewpoint of Self, the consciousness covers all viewpoints, in other words all lives.

What is the purpose of life?

The answer is simple, but it doesn't please everyone.

Mankind has for a long time pondered over the purpose of life. The purpose has mostly been searched for in the wrong place. That is why it hasn't been found.

Since the insight of this knowledge is very central for the real self-knowledge of the person, the lack of it makes him unstable and he can with false arguments be brought to a self perception and state of will that is untruthful, and prevent him from experiencing his own real self.

This situation suits those who desire power, since there only is power when people accept to live in accordance with the images of reality offered by those who hold the power. The real purpose doesn't please those who desire power, since it doesn't favor the binding of the person into their control. As a matter of fact, it will exclude outer control from the person's life.

There are many religions that offer images of reality about the purpose of life. However, most of them are beautiful empty pictures and they are used like politics to mislead people from themselves.

The purpose of life, from the individual's viewpoint, is actually a very simple and easily solved problem.

The person has since birth had a will, born out of Self, that is the purpose of his life. This will contains the full answer to his purpose, in other words the purpose of his life. This will defines the reason to his existence and it is born out of himself.

The fulfillment of this will is the life purpose of the person and the only real satisfaction is born out of its fulfillment, since its fulfillment is the fulfillment of Self's intention, the fulfillment of the purpose of life.

The fulfillment of the original will is functionality of life.

What is the fundamental reason?

The fundamental purpose of bodies is to be preserved, that is to be nourished enough and to reproduce. Based on this argument we could say that the fundamental reason is survival.

If we observe the matter this way, then any action that strengthens the ability to survive is a good one. This way of observing might grow selfishness and self-centricity.

Since we are not bodies, the purpose of life can't be sought for on the body level. The purpose of life is in our desire to create and have experiences. Without this reason there wouldn't be life and if this reason is prevented, then the motivation and will to live is lost. If this reason gets more space, then the joy of life and motivation grows.

The reason to the existence of life is our desire to create, our desire to fulfill life with its original purpose, in other words as the expression of our own free wills. That is the original reason for the material existence, and without it this existence wouldn't even exist.

Seen from the viewpoint of the being, which is Self, it is quite insignificant what kind of life form or life it maintains, as long as it is based on its own choice.

Ultimately we all experience all lives from the viewpoint of the all-connection, in other words seen from the viewpoint of the real Self. This viewpoint can't be experienced from the consciousness of the limited existence, but it makes it easier to understand the whole.

The only thing with importance to the individual's life is that it follows his original idea, in other words his will.

It is his individual reason and his part of fulfilling the entirety. It is the basic demand for the quality and the reason of life. It is the reason he himself has chosen. It is his individual viewpoint, which is directly connected to the entirety. It is not a detached phenomenon.

What are parents?

The parents are the closest link in the chain of mankind.

Parenting is a promise of help and guiding to the beginning of life for the child.

The parents are usually also biologically the child's closest link in the chain of mankind.

Father- and motherhood, in a biological sense, is related only to the child's biological inheritance. For the child, the spiritual value of biological parenthood is on an imaginary level, not real. The history of the body affects us only on behalf of the physical inheritance.

Father- and motherhood, in a spiritual sense, is the most significant source to the child when he is creating his first viewpoint, this is also the most genuine parenthood. This parenthood is in a significant position in relation to the life of the child.

The parents are guides to the start of life, in other words the central source to the child's first viewpoint.

The parents aren't the only guides in the child's life. A child looks for different things from different persons in accordance with the needs of the progress of his own will. The parents are not, and neither do they have to be the answer to all needs.

The foundation of the child's life is strongly affected by the parent's skill as guides. All parents aren't good guides. Hardly anyone is perfect, but it can't even be expected of anyone. We have to remember, that as long as the world isn't perfect, there won't be any perfect parents.

In time the child has to take responsibility for the effects the parent's flaws and mistakes had on his own person. Then it is good if the child understands that these mistakes weren't invented by his parents, or the product of ill will. The parents are only the closest link in a long chain of mistakes.

Those are the mistakes his parents didn't manage to correct. What is essential is that as few mistakes as possible are passed on.

The child's relation to his parents is always a dependent relationship, but not necessarily a relationship that contains real nearness. It contains as much nearness as the communication between them provides it.

The child has not any obligations towards his parents, that in relation to them obliges him to anything over his own will, in other words the purpose created by Self.

There is not anything in the world that can truthfully be placed over Self. Anything that is placed over the own fundamental will of the person, is suffocating his purpose of life and is therefore of a great harm to his life.

What are children?

The children are free born beginnings of their own wills.

A child is a new thought.

The children are the new thoughts that the development of mankind requires.

The children are the future. Each own will expresses this new thought.

A child is not a messenger of traditions, or the past.

The child has an own will already at birth. He's got a will born out of Self, which defines the entire idea of his life. Everyone who is born has this will. Everyone's own original will is good.

Childhood is a state of body and mind. Self is unchanging, regardless if it is a question of children or adults. The only things changing are the states of the mind and body.

The child's only responsibility is to grow up to be himself, that is to be the fulfiller of the own will that was created by Self. All other claimed responsibilities are lies.

The child's role is to grow from the viewpoints of his environment towards being the fulfiller of his own will. Childhood is a time of preparation. It contains a lot of learning, participation and work.

It is natural for a child that he wants to participate in all kinds of doing, and to be interested of learning new things. This feature disappears only when he doesn't get good enough guiding in the direction of his own will.

Guiding in the direction of the own will is guidance that takes into consideration the striving that rises from the child himself. As well as the child really has been heard can he, to the best of ability, be helped to that direction.

The child grows in the direction of the guiding to the viewpoint of his guides. He hardly criticizes or doubts the guiding. At the very beginning he copies everything, also a lot of what the guides wouldn't want to pass on from themselves or their own being. Gradually he starts to choose what he takes and what he doesn't take.

The problems created by the guiding, or the influence of the world in common, can't really be seen before the child starts approaching adulthood. At this stage the child experiences a need to approach independent action and that might lead to conflicts with his environment, since the environment tries to keep the child a child, and the child wants to change the child into an adult.

To the extent the child grows apart from Self and his own will, he will feel bad when the growth of distance starts to be of significance for his life.

At start it doesn't really have an effect, since his will isn't yet in the stage of fulfilling. It starts to have an effect when he tries to fulfill his life. If he then has inadequate knowledge or skills, he will feel pain. What he wants to do, won't be fulfilled with the equipment he's got.

If the child at that stage has lost his contact to Self, he won't feel pain due to the distance to Self and his original will. The possible pain he feels is born out of the distance to an imaginary will. In that case it is a question of that he doesn't meet the ideas of some adopted, but in fact to himself alien values of good and right. However, a bit deeper under the surface there still exists a desire to reach Self and the own will.

The connection to Self and the own will can be lost, but the values created in their place can never replace the spiritual well-being, that only comes out of the fulfillment of the original will.

The purpose that replaces the own will isn't the fulfillment of the own life, it is the fulfillment of another life.

If a child loses his connection to Self and his own original will, he will lose his only genuine life, and becomes a puppet in something else than the life he intended to live.

Self

I am

Self is the deepest selfhood. Self is the center of selfhood that never changes.

Each and everyone has changed during his life, and everyone can make the discovery, that the experience of the central self-perception has remained the same nevertheless. That consciousness is Self. Its understanding can be deepened and the consciousness of it can be grown.

Self is the one who knows it exists. Self is the one that is.

I am not

Self isn't a thought, or the body.

The human learns ideas from his environment while he is growing up. He copies these thoughts to be able to be a part of the reality he was born to. The environment doesn't confirm his real selfhood, but educates him to believe in a selfhood that is formed of the body and thoughts.

He copies a thought, in accordance with his own understanding, from the environment and places it in his mind. This thought is a picture in which he, in accordance to the given instructions, tries to place his sense of self.

While growing up, the human strengthens his sense of self in the picture he himself created. He might try to find his real self, but usually he looks for the selfhood in the picture in question. He might try to change what he experiences to be himself in what he thinks is a better direction, in which case he changes that picture to the extent possible.

For some people the connection to the true selfhood is preserved so that they are aware of its existence, but the imaginary selfhood is still strong.

The first step to find selfhood

The first step to find selfhood is to locate selfhood, or should we say to understand what selfhood is not.

When a human is talking about his body, he expresses it by saying "my body". This expression contains the thought that selfhood owns the body, but that selfhood isn't the body.

The person can observe his body part by part and discover that none of those parts are the selfhood, or even a part of the selfhood.

Thoughts are not selfhood. If the person observes his thoughts, it is not difficult for him to notice that selfhood is the one observing, not what is being observed. When the person thinks, he rotates thoughts, in other words images in his mind, which isn't selfhood either but the place where thoughts are kept.

By observing this way one can quite easily get a hang of that selfhood is solely and exclusively the consciousness that knows it exists.

If the person wants to start freeing himself from the world's thought, the general ideas that he has learned, then the first step is to improve the insight of selfhood. The stronger understanding of selfhood the person has, the easier it is for him to confront and change his conception of reality.

The Self-nearing exercise

A very simple exercise helps one to understand Self and to strengthen the experience of it.

In this exercise the person sits comfortably in a chair, in which it is easy to relax. He closes his eyes and concentrates only on experiencing himself. He doesn't think or strive anywhere, and he doesn't follow anything that comes up in his mind. The only thing he does is concentrating to experience himself. He doesn't think about it, he only experiences.

The exercise might as well be done lying down, but then it is easier to fall asleep. At start falling asleep happens more easily, but it is nothing to worry about all too much. If one falls asleep, then one falls asleep, the exercise progresses in any case. Falling asleep this way is very good rest, so it gives benefits anyway.

Falling asleep can't be avoided, and there is no point in trying to avoid it too much. With time the falling asleep comes later and eventually it will disappear.

The recommended exercise is one hour per day. If there isn't a possibility to do that, then a quite good exercise can be carried out in half an hour. If one hour feels too hard at start, then one can perfectly well start off with half an hour exercises.

The exercise can be done multiple times a day, in periods of one to two hours. If multiple exercises are carried out in a day, it is good to have pauses between the exercises and do something that strengthens the connection to the surrounding world.

Any kind of focus on the material world works well as a strengthener of the connection. For example looking at material items, touching them and doing something related to the items is effective.

This exercise is very flexible regarding the number of exercises, but it is good if one tries to be able to carry out a one hour exercise every day.

For the sake of the exercise it is best if its duration is free. Then the person rises up from the exercise without any outer stimuli and in his own time, when the exercise is done. For example using a clock to announce when an hour has passed is a less good alternative, than if one learns to rise up from the exercise by oneself when a full hour has passed.

The completion time of the exercise where one rise up in one's own time, times up with the progress of the exercise. Then it can sometimes last longer, if there is reason for it. It can also last for a shorter time.

Regardless of all its simplicity, this exercise is a quite powerful strengthener of selfhood. To support his exercise, the person should have a good basic knowledge of the inner reality, since it supports the understanding of selfhood.

Responsibility

Responsibility for the own will

There is only one genuine responsibility.

The only responsibility in life for each and everyone is to fulfill Self, to fulfill the own will. All other claimed responsibilities are lies.

The understanding of the own will is the first prerequisite for this responsibility.

Confrontation, the corner stone of responsibility

To confront is to observe the matter until it can be seen clearly. The confrontation of matters is the corner stone of responsibility.

The confrontation can produce pain to the person and it can be hard. The person has to be able to continue the confrontation regardless of the pain, since otherwise he gives up and stops confronting, in which case he can't approach the matter.

He can do this only because he chooses to lie to himself instead of that he would approach his real selfhood by confronting the lies that prevent him from it. Only lies separate the person from his real selfhood and all lies are maintained by himself.

The ability to confront grows with the growth of consciousness. Raising and clearing the level of consciousness strengthens the consciousness of Self, and therefore the Self-nearing exercise is one of the key factors when growing the ability to confront.

Confrontation is not to accept any offered truths, it is not to submit to anything, and it is not to believe in anything.

In the frames of the world's thought people are suggested to confront reality such as the world's thought defines it, and as the world's thought wants to keep it. It can for example be called facing facts. In that case it isn't a question of confrontation, but submission, which is irresponsibility. It is submitting to accept an image of reality that is built on lies.

One needs to get free of building one's life by submitting to the world's thought in this way, even if the world couldn't be changed to ones liking. Its lie has to be confronted thoroughly.

If one for practical reasons has to accept that the world right now works as it works, the ground for that choice has to be the own free will. The person sees it to be a practical choice, since any other choice wouldn't be functional. He is also free to change it instantly, when it is possible.

He is no longer submitted to it, it is only a question of choice for him. Besides that, he is freer to see how it really works.

Taking responsibility

The only obstacle to taking responsibility is lying to oneself, which is irresponsibility. It is inner dishonesty.

The person lies to himself when he maintains a thought that isn't true enough and claims to himself that it is true enough. Each thought has to be true enough for the need in that moment, compared to the own will.

It can be very difficult for the person to notice in what way he lies to himself, even if he is aware of that he does so.

The less aware the person is of himself, the harder it is for him to notice that he lies to himself. It is a matter of an insufficient level of consciousness.

If something doesn't function, then there is an error in the presumed facts. If there is no error, things will function as expected.

Life isn't functioning if it doesn't make progress in the wanted direction, which is always the direction of the original own will, its strengthening and fulfilling.

When life doesn't function, it is time to confront the reasons to its non-functionality. The reasons always lay in the ignorance of the person, which is weakness of the level of consciousness.

Ignorance is an irresponsible condition, and it is corrected by confronting the lies that prevent one from seeing flawlessly. Flawless seeing is to see the sufficient truth so clear, that the intended can be fulfilled the way it is wanted.

For the person to be able to confront the ideas that contain an error, in other words a lie, he must be conscious enough of himself. If his consciousness of himself is on a lower level than the incorrect idea, he can't reveal the error to himself.

Nothing is endlessly true enough, since life is continuing motion, and the need set by its challenge constantly grows. Therefore the person always needs better and better insights about matters. What was enough yesterday, isn't enough today.

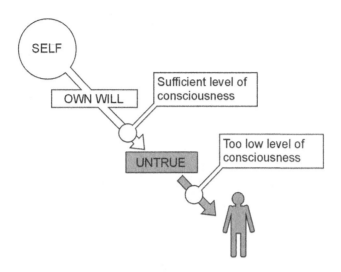

In the picture above, there are two places that display the level of consciousness. The other is a sufficient level of consciousness and the other is a too low level of consciousness. The levels of consciousness are viewpoints that the person has chosen. He observes the matter from the chosen viewpoint and he experiences reality from that viewpoint.

The situation described by the picture exists, when some idea isn't true enough compared to the level required by the person's own will in that moment.

Often the person, in his viewpoint, can't understand that he is lying to himself, since he doesn't do it consciously. This doesn't change the fact that he is lying to himself, since Self is always aware of everything. Self has to make sure that the viewpoint of the own life rises enough for the lies to be revealed.

When the level of consciousness is too low, the person can't reveal the lie he is maintaining to himself. He has to rise in consciousness above the lie, for him to be able to see what is lie in it.

When the viewpoint's level of consciousness is lower than the level needed to reveal the lie, the lie can't be seen, since the person experiences the lie to be true. Because of this, the raising of the viewpoint's level of consciousness is inevitable.

When the level of consciousness is too low, the person maintains something that isn't true enough as a life-controlling factor.

There is nothing such in the person's mind that he didn't place there himself, and there is nothing such that he doesn't maintain himself. There is nothing such that anyone else could remove. He is the only one who can remove anything from there.

The removal happens with insights. When the person sees a lie, its influence ceases at the depth of the insight the person had.

For insights it isn't enough with a truth suggested by an outer instance, and which the person accepts, even if it would be true. The person himself must see what is really there. It is the only way to truly cleanse the mind. An idea suggested by someone else doesn't help, even if it would be accurate. Without a self performed insight, that which needs do happen doesn't happen.

In this world the usual try to help a person who is confused is by the helpers "truth", which is based on thinking and which attempts to help the person to adjust to the world's thought. Seen from the person's viewpoint, it is a completely wrong direction.

Adjusting to the world's thought can reduce the confusion, if the person to the same extent abandons his real self. If the person doesn't abandon his real self, then the help to adjust to the world's thought will confuse him even more.

Self creates chaos

Self can try to find ways to move its person in the desired way, but doesn't necessarily succeed with that, since other instances also influence the person. The other instances are those persons, who appeal to the world's thought. Those world's thoughts that the person himself maintains in his mind also have an influence on him. In other words he considers them to be true, or then he considers something that forces him to accept their influence to be true.

Self can, if it wants to, drive his person into trouble just because it wants to break the effect of the lies, and to find a better way to reach the person it wants to create. The person isn't necessarily aware of this at all.

This driving into trouble happens simply by that Self strengthens the flow of the own will. This grows the awareness of it in the person's viewpoint, and it also grows the demand. The person's viewpoint is shaken and its clarity weakens.

A confused person will create problems for himself. Usually the problems are born gradually, but they can appear like a bolt from the blue just when the person experiences everything to be well.

The purpose of the problems is to get the person to approach Self, in other words to abandon his untruthful world. This requires a change of the viewpoint, and it can only be solved by confronting the lies that prevent the person from his own will.

The solution to the problems is to raise the level of truth, which means that the person has to reveal to himself the lies that he himself maintains. In this context, solution means that the person approaches himself.

The person could strive towards the world's thought and find balance there, but it doesn't solve the actual problem ever. Then the problem actually gets worse, since the distance to the own self grows. That means it isn't solving the problem, but avoiding the problem by lying to oneself even more, which is to lower the consciousness.

A human who moves from one chaos to another in his life, is precisely in that kind of situation. He is in a bad position in the sense that he doesn't manage to solve the problem, but in a good position in the sense that he hasn't lost his connection to himself.

It is a more responsible condition than to submit to the world's thought, if we compare to the relation between the person and Self. Looking from the viewpoint of life, it is a bad condition, if the person can't manage to solve it in a way where approaching of Self happens and the condition of the person becomes clear.

Untruthful responsibilities

People have as a custom to teach the person what his responsibilities are according to the world's thought. Not a single one of them is based on the truth, but they are lies.

Some of the responsibilities the person is taught to be his responsibilities are such that it is easier to accept them than to oppose them, but it would still be self-deception to consider them to be true. For the person to be able to approach his own real will, he must see even through these lies. The approaching of the own will and Self requires understanding of all the lies.

The responsibilities he can get free from after understanding them to be lies, he will gladly give up, regardless of what others might think about it. The responsibilities he can't get free from are very few, and usually their maintainer is the state or some other societal organ.

Some responsibilities are such that he wants to choose them himself, in other words to keep them. Even regarding them, he must find the lie they contain. In that case the lie can be found in the reason of the responsibility, which is a reason of an outer will, not a reason of his own will.

He has to disassemble such a responsibility so that the outer reason ceases, and after that he can take the responsibility for reasons defined by his own will. Then his viewpoint regarding the matter is correct and he is free.

The truth

The truth is the practical truth

The truth is relative.

Any argument can be said to be true.

The truth is relative, in other words any argument is true on some level. However, we can't call any other argument true, besides one that is true enough compared to the need.

Naturally there also exists the absolute truth, but it is not essential from the viewpoint of our life.

When we speak of the truth, we always speak of the relative truth, if not something else is specifically mentioned. It is the only practical truth.

The truth is multi-leveled, essential is to find the right level of truth compared to what it is applied to. If it functions, it is true enough. If it doesn't function, it is not the kind of truth that would be enough for that situation. It can be quite true, but it isn't sufficiently true.

The other option is that the truth in question exceeds the level that should be used, and its functionality is low. Functionality is optimization between the result and the effort.

For every object the most suitable level is the level of truth where the object is. Other levels are impractical, or they won't even function.

TOO HIGH	
UNNECESSARY HIGH	
RIGHT LEVEL	LEVEL OF THE OBJECT
WEAK LEVEL	
TOO LOW	

The truth is very unconditional

The black and white in this context means that some argument either is true or not true. When it is true, then it is completely true on the level of truth in question. If it is not, then it is not true. It can be quite true, or a little true, or far away from true, but it is not in any case completely true, in other words it can't be held true.

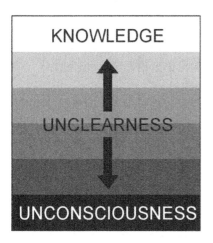

Knowledge is clear for one who knows. He sees the full area clearly on the intended level. If he doesn't see it completely clearly, he doesn't see it precisely as it is and he needs to observe the area until all the unclearness is gone.

The level of unconsciousness in relation to some knowledge is that the person has no connection to it.

When the person sees the truth, he sees it completely clearly and it is black and white, it is not gray. The image of reality is gray when the person can't see what is true. He is either incapable of seeing it, or he doesn't want to see it.

Offering gray in the shape of truth is often used for the most various reasons. The reason is the incapability to see the truth, or in the desire to hide what is true from oneself or others.

Grayness in often used to patch up holes in untrue thought models, or to maintain wishful images. The human is very tempted towards the gray, since it can feel easier to accept than the truth.

The truth can feel scary and it can feel hard. Scary because the own conception of the world can break by its foundation due to the understanding of the truth. Hard because the own thought-images of good and right can be in conflict with the truth.

The human easily chooses to defend the good and right according to his existing concept of reality instead of that he would start changing his ideas, even though the understanding of good and right requires the understanding of the truth.

The truth is not the purpose, the truth is a tool

The search for the truth can be held as search for the truth only when the focus of the person is in approaching Self. If that isn't in question, the experience of achieved clearness isn't true, but only imaginary clearness of a limited reality.

Limited reality in this context is the kind of reality that is divergent or misleads from the need of Self's purpose. Unlimited reality on the other hand is represented by the freedom of movement in accordance with the needs of Self's goals.

The seeker of truth can't settle in limited realities, he needs to be open to the limitless. Genuine truth isn't in a closed space, it is infinite.

Due to the relativity of the truth, we always have gray areas in our view of life. The grey areas are a part of our development. When we get something cleared on some level, in other words we reach the truth on that level, a new area opens up for us, and that area is the truth on a higher level. It is gray in our eyes, since we can't see it clearly. It is not true for us, we have just grown aware of the existence of a higher level.

The movement in the changing landscape of clearness and unclearness is intense until we reach an adequate level of truth, seen from the viewpoint of our own will. When we reach that, our development normalizes, and we are fully functional on the level that was the basic requirement for the fulfilling of our will.

At start, the need of clearing the truth is great and the clarifying becomes the central function of life. We have no reason to strive towards active action before we are on such a level, that we can carry out our own will from an adequate level, seen from its viewpoint.

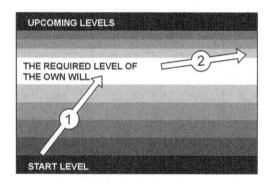

At start (arrow 1. in the picture) the need to reach the right level of action is dominant. After that (arrow 2. in the picture) the raising of the level is part of fulfilling the own purpose.

When we reach such a level where our own will's requirements for action are met, our focus moves automatically from clearing the basic problems to the fulfilling of the thought of our own life. Then we're no longer in a direct emergency considering our own will, and the need for clearing our view normalizes. It becomes a part of our life, it is no longer our whole life.

The reason for seeking the truth is always expediency, it is not seeking the truth for the truth. The truth is sought for us to be able to carry out what was meant to be done. The intensity at start is caused by the lack of truth, by the distance between the condition of the person and the purpose of the own will. When this lack is corrected, the focus moves to the fulfilling.

It is a question of fulfilling the own will, fulfilling the own purpose of life and opening the required level of truth, so that it can be used. From that forth the seeking of truth is dictated by the needs of the own will.

The truth is independent of us

The truth is what it is.

The truth is what it is, fully independent of what we wish it would be. The human has a great tendency to set terms, in accordance with his thought-images, for the truth when he tries to see it. As if our own ideas of propriety, or our wishes of appropriateness, somehow would have an effect on that which is true.

The human fears the truth and the effect it would have if it comes out. Therefore he sets terms for what it can be to be accepted. As if the truth somehow would have a need for the acceptance of humans. The only consequence of this is that the human can't see it. This is a tragicomic phenomenon, but very normal for the human.

It is, however, quite easy to understand, that our opinions don't have an effect on the truth, and that our wishes won't change it. It is coldly just what it is.

The truth can't be reached when holding on to lies. No terms can be set for what the truth can be. The truth will not change to anything else for our sake. It is what it is.

The truth is simple

The truth is simple by its nature.

When something presented is true, it is functional, and when it is understood, it is simple and clear.

Complexity is lowness of the level of consciousness, and confusion.

Thought models that are based on lies and inadequate truth are complicated by nature.

Thought models that are based on lies are complicated, since they function on the thought level in consciousness, in other words on a very low level.

For them non-functionality is characteristic, because in order to hide lies one must add endlessly many explanations and thoughts to patch up the non-functionality of the lie.

They are like an incorrectly constructed house on which, for it to remain standing up, one must add endlessly many supporting structures and it still won't be any good.

An own chapter are the thought structures that are presented as functional and are held for functional, but their functionality in reality is in fact weak. Then the idea of their functionality lives its own reality separated life in peoples mind.

It is characteristic for thoughts based on lies to require belief instead of understanding. Belief is often covered up with a cloak of knowledge in such a way that some arguments are believed to be knowledge, even if they are not true.

Complexity sometimes acts as a good protection, since with that one can create a thought-image of that the presenter of the thought knows much.

Vocabulary can also be used as protection, and with it one can create an impression of knowledge, even if it only is a question of a chatter of words.

Regardless of everything they are untruthful, since they are not true at all, or they are not true enough to function.

When seeking for insight, it is good to be aware of that when the confusion decreases and the clearness grows, one is approaching the insight that opens up the knowledge to the level that is pursued. The reaching of insight in accordance with the level the seeker is looking for, is for the seeker himself a clear and simple experience.

The higher the level of consciousness is in question, the more simple things become. Presenting a viewpoint from a high level is difficult on lower levels, since it can't be fully expressed on lower levels of consciousness.

It can be described, but for the receiver to be able to understand the described, the receiver must reach it through insights. The needed insights can be facilitated by building descriptions stepwise in such matter, that the closest level is near enough for the receiver.

The fulfilling of a high level of consciousness can be difficult regardless of its simplicity, since all fulfilling is ultimately born out of communication.

The absolute truth

The absolute doesn't have any distance to anything.

The absolute truth is a point.

The absolute truth is unconditional all-knowing.

Seen from the viewpoint of the absolute truth the observer has no distance to anything. For him the universes and all possible existing is a point that has no dimensions. Not in time, space or any other dimension. For him everything is there.

It is so far away from us, that it doesn't exist for us in other than a theoretical sense. To ponder over it isn't essential from the viewpoint of life, and not even meaningful.

When speaking of truth in Alkuajatus, it doesn't mean the absolute truth, if it isn't specifically mentioned.

In Alkuajatus the purpose and the value of the definition of the absolute truth is in its use as a reference point to understand the levels of truth.

The lie

The lie

Lie is distance.

Lie creates distance and maintains it.

Lie is distance from the absolute truth.

The lie is relative, as is the truth.

Any argument that differs from the absolute truth can be seen as a lie.

Lie is the precondition of existence. This is the practical lie.

Lie is an insufficient truth. It is any argument, that isn't sufficiently true in relation to the purpose. This is the relative lie.

When speaking of the lie in Alkuajatus, we speak of the relative lie, if the context doesn't show that it means the absolute lie or the practical lie.

The characteristic of the lie is that it reduces freedom.

The purpose of the lie is to conceal the truth.

All unclearness in relation to something is based on lies, which conceal the truth from the person. To approach the truth is to reveal those lies.

The idea of the lie

The idea of the lie is to create distance and maintain it. Distance creates finiteness.

The practical lie

The practical lie is the maintainer of the intended distance.

Without the lie we would be in the absolute, since there would be no distances at all. Then the world wouldn't exist, since the existence of the world requires existence of distances.

Without distances there are no viewpoints, which are what the world consists of. This lie of existence is an expedient distance from the truth. Therefore it can be called a practical lie.

The lie that maintains existence is expedient. It is a part of life and the existence of the world. It is a state of finiteness in accordance with the intention.

The practical lie is individual. Each and everyone is on an expedient level of finiteness, in other words a level of consciousness, when he is free.

The purpose of the lie that maintains the existence is not to be a permanent condition. It is a chosen starting point, from where the journey to find the truth is started. This can be called the growth of consciousness.

The final destination is the absolute truth, and when the being has reached it, it can choose a new, lowered consciousness to gain a new experience.

The lowered state of consciousness doesn't concern the being itself, it concerns the person it creates. The being transports its person through the levels of consciousness and experiences the viewpoints of its person on his journey towards perfection.

This journey towards a higher truth, in other words the growth of consciousness, goes through the disassembling of lies.

The lie as a misleader

The lie is used to maintain a greater distance than the free will intends.

A lie that doesn't concern enabling the original limited existence of the world, is a lie that someone has created with the intention to be able to control someone else.

The idea of that lie is to create distance to the level of truth intended by Self. It is used to prevent the fulfillment of the own original will and the existence of free will.

Relativity of the lie

Lie is unconsciousness in relation to the absolute truth, in other words distance from the absolute truth.

Some argument is a lie to the person, if it prevents him from approaching a level of truth that is in accordance with his intention.

When a person reaches some level of truth and it is a sufficient truth in that moment, then it is true seen from his viewpoint, in other words it is the practical truth that was mentioned earlier.

When his need grows to require something that is more true, the previously reached level of truth becomes insufficient and is then a lie in relation to the person, it is no longer the truth.

A practical lie is the truth, when it maintains the intended state of finiteness. When it prevents one from reaching the intended level of truth, then it is a lie in relation to the intention.

The misleading lies are also relative. A misleading lie that doesn't prevent one from reaching the intended level of truth is not a too great lie, and therefore it doesn't have to be solved in that moment. Then the misleading lie is a practical lie, seen from the person's viewpoint, since it is a part of his intended state of finiteness in just that moment.

Similarly, a practical lie that is below the person's level of consciousness can be seen as a misleading lie, since accepting it would lead in the wrong direction, in other words it would lower the consciousness.

To overcome all lies the person must raise his level of truth so that he reaches a sufficient level of truth, and finds the practical truth in accordance with his intention.

The absolute lie

Matter is the absolute lie. The lowest point of lie is that the being believes itself to be matter in unconsciousness, in which case its freedom of movement is zero. It is the opposite of the absolute truth.

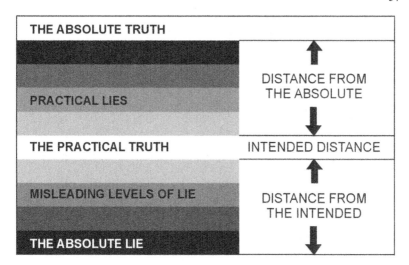

The force of the lie

Lie and unanimity

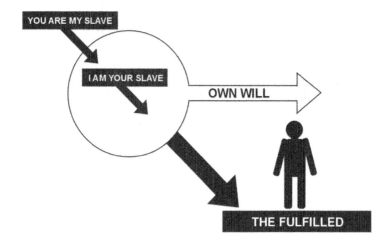

The force of the lie is in the person's own acceptance.

In his mind, there is unanimity with the argument of the lie. When there from the outside comes a lie that tries to control his life, he looks in his mind and in there is the same argument, which he himself maintains.

The consequence is that he experiences the lie to be true, and acts in accordance with it.

This condition is quite common in society. The basic thoughts maintained by society were taught already as a child, and the person didn't evaluate their accuracy at that time, but accepted them without questioning.

Full unanimity is such where the person holds an argument to be a self-evident truth that he doesn't question, and it doesn't even come to mind to question it.

The problem with self-evident truths, in other words the lies that are held for truths, is that revealing them can be difficult, since it doesn't even come to the person's mind to question them.

If the person starts raising his level of consciousness, then all of these to self-evident formed lies will be revealed at some point, since the person's level of consciousness strives above them.

No lie has a definitive safe haven in the person's mind. The lies that are held to be self-evident truths will be found and they will fall. Nobody is definitively under the force of any lie.

Lie and counter-thought

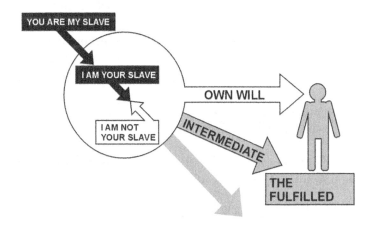

When the person starts questioning the truthfulness of the offered lie, the first reaction is to argue against it and to try to prevent the effect of the lie. The person creates a counter-argument and prevents the effect of the lie with it.

The counter-argument requires the use of force in the mind, whereby another thought is born in the mind, and it opposes the thought that was there earlier. Both of these thoughts are maintained by the person himself. This means that he creates both the subjecting thought and its counter-thought.

With the counter-thought the effect of the lie is prevented, but it doesn't fully solve the problem. The person isn't free in that condition. He can correct his path of movement to some extent, but he doesn't free it.

This condition is better that the previous condition, from the viewpoint of life, but for the seeker of freedom this is only an intermediate stage. At this intermediate stage the person has a conflict that wears him inside of him.

This intermediate stage of revealing the lie is very commonly a permanent condition. It might be so, because people usually don't know that it only is an intermediate stage. It is not a fully conducted freeing from the lie. Because of this, there can be many of those in the person's mind and they wear him immensely.

This intermediate stage is related to the distance table that is discussed in the chapter "Distances", passage "anger".

In this condition, the lie still has an influence on the person and therefore power in the person's life.

This intermediate stage can be softened by reducing the counter-thought and using abandoning. More of that in the chapter "Abandoning".

Disappearance of the force of lie

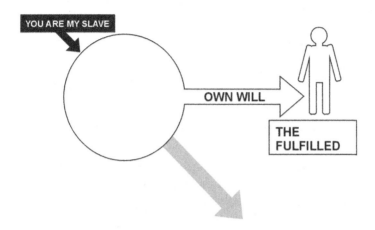

The lie has an influence on the person's actions as long as the person himself maintains unanimity with the argument of the lie. When the person fully reveals the lie, its influence disappears completely and the person is free in relation to that lie. He stops maintaining it in his own mind.

Disassembling of the unanimity doesn't occur by thinking, it occurs only by that the person sees it completely. This means that the person's level of consciousness and his understanding of the lie are sufficient for him to see what it is, and why it isn't true.

The disassembling of each thought requires that the person's viewpoint is above the thought in question. If it isn't above it, then the person holds it for a self-evident truth and isn't capable of questioning it.

An insufficient view leaves force to the lie and it influences the mind, and of course life in a weakening way, until it is completely revealed.

When the person starts raising his level of consciousness in general, it leads to the revealing of all lies, since his eyes gradually opens up to see what is true and what is not. In this sense the seeker of truth is on a safe path, in other words a path where the force of the lies weakens and the truth wins. The truth can only win.

When revealing the lies, the most excellent tool is their observation without thinking. The person can study things and try to find truth in what they are, and what is true instead. To reveal a lie he must have insight, not create new images of the matter.

Insight doesn't occur by thinking, but by looking. Thinking is rotating of images that are in the mind, and the knowledge they themselves contain won't solve them. They must be observed, not used. The better the observation happens without thinking, the more effective it is.

If we return to the example presented in the picture, the object of observation in the mind is the thought "I am your slave", in other words the thought that creates unanimity. If a counter-thought has been created, it must also be observed so that one notices it to be a counter-thought and sees it.

Then the observation happens in a way where one looks at the thought "I am your slave" for so long, that the lie in it is noticed. It might be connected to other thoughts that support it. They will all gradually rise up to the mind and their force will also weaken.

When the thought "I am your slave" is fully confronted, it simply disappears. The observation must be conducted by observing only that thought. One mustn't be of any opinion about it, and not create any counter-thoughts against it, but calmly observe it and see it. The possible pain caused by it must be received, and the observation mustn't be stopped because of the pain.
When the observation is calmly continued, the force of the thought weakens and at some point it will lose its force

completely. When the person gets an insight about that lie, it will disappear for good. If it doesn't disappear for good, it hasn't been fully confronted.

Insight is not that one understands it to be a lie with the help of logical thinking. It doesn't disappear by thinking, it disappears by looking at it for a sufficiently long time without any thought about it. By thinking one only develops the thought structures further, and doesn't disassemble them as purposed.

Lies, averages and the truth

The average of lies

In life it is very common that one first listens to different views, and then tries to make some sort of average of them, by one's mind. But the fact is that by doing this, one can't achieve anything else but an untruthful average. The truth isn't the average of differences between views. While observing the truth there is one point on which the focus should be put. As well as it has been reached, as well one has understood that which is true.

Let us in this context remember, that Alkuajatus deals with the truth as a matter that means the needed level of the own will. All such that decreases the clearness of the own will and weakens its fulfilling is lie, in other words too far away from the sufficient truth.

Picture: "L1" = Lie 1, "L2" = Lie 2, "A" = Average and "T" = Truth

The arrows illustrate directions and the circles distances from the truth. The average "A" is positioned in a point that is the average between the distances and the directions on the arch.

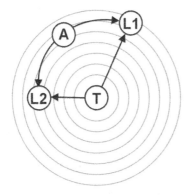

When we listen to thoughts that concern life and that aren't true, we listen to lies about life. If we believe them, we can't remain in our own thought about what we are going to do in our life.

If we listen to the arguments L1 and L2 to create a picture of the matter, we will easily end up with an average result A. Then we might feel that we have listened to everyone and considered the different views.

As a matter of fact, we don't then take responsibility for that which is true, but we collect untruths and are in accordance with our learned patterns understanding, tolerant and why not also modern as well. At the same time we leave without attention the only thing we should consider, in other words the truth.

If we think about the matter based on the previous picture, we can see that believing in L2 we would be closer to the truth. Therefore our average idea of the truth is actually more untrue than one of the offered lies.

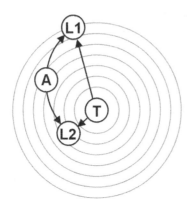

In this picture L2 is quite near the truth, and if it is closer to the truth than the observer himself, it will even help him to approach the truth, even if its accuracy won't last all the way. The average "A" is considerably further away from the truth and because of that, it is misleading compared to L2. L1 on the other hand is very far away from the truth.

Mankind has been led astray with lies, and people's willingness to make average ideas of the truth serves well those who want to lead astray. When the lie is grown, people can be made to move further away from the truth, since people try to create average ideas of matters.

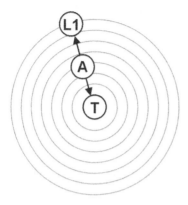

In this picture, we compare the damage caused by the average made between the truth and the lie. In this picture, the person himself has a good touch to the truth. If he yields with the world's thoughts and makes averages to please one or several persons, he himself will distance himself from what is true instead of remaining in the truth. This option might feel tempting in certain circumstances.

This might occur when the person doesn't want to remain in the truth, or demand the approach of the truth, to be able to avoid some conflict with some person. If the situation is random, not permanent, then it could be practical. Every passer-by won't cause that the person is prevented from being his own self, even if he in that situation would accept an average idea, or even a lie.

If the relation to the person is permanent, then the creating of an average idea is precisely as harmful as the relationship is fixed for the person. The fixity does that the person must constantly remain in the average idea, and he isn't free to approach the truth and his own will in the way he is supposed to.

His own living space will shrink, and his freedom of movement is restrained. Then the nearness isn't true, it only feels that way as long as the person lies to himself. He doesn't want to see that which is true, since then the illusion of nearness would break. While he is lying to himself, he is also lying to others.

Restraining things might be human relations, imaginary love, money, position or anything such that the person values or longs for so much, that he is ready to lie to himself because of it. Some restraining things might be tremendously difficult for the person to overcome, yet he must free himself from them.

All restraining things are in fact built out of lies. Their restraining force isn't in the truth, but in some lie that the person hasn't yet revealed to himself. He can't yet see the lie that restrains him. If he would see it, then that lie wouldn't have any power over him.

Even if he would experience the abandoning of the restraining images to be difficult, possibly even impossible, he doesn't have a choice. Only by abandoning them will he advance in approaching the truth. Sometimes it is painful, but when it is done, and one succeeds in getting free of the restraining illusions, one will never regret abandoning them. Before the abandoning, the person might experience that he will lose something really important.

If one intends to approach the truth, in other words the own will's level of truth, one can in every situation only choose the ideas that are as close to the truth as possible, and that serves the growth of truth in the best possible way.

Abandoning difficult things will get easier if the person has an own experience of abandoning, in other words of to have let go of some lies and after that been freed of their chains. Even if the experience concerns a small matter, the mechanics of abandoning is exactly the same.

The truth will never forgive anything because it feels difficult or impossible. The truth is what it is, and it won't move anywhere for our sakes, for any reason. Our possibility to reach the truth is solely and exclusively in confronting it such as it is.

The truth isn't an average.

The truth is cold to the one who doesn't want to see it, and a warm friend to the one who knows it.

Human relations

Caring

Caring for others is the being's natural relation to others.

Caring is love, it is truth and free flow between the beings.

Love

Love is nearness in spirit.

Love is nearness that is born out of good communication.

Good communication is honest and open flow.

Honesty is freedom from lies, which always starts with honesty towards oneself. If the person isn't fully open and honest to himself, he can't be that to others. The seed of lie is in dishonesty to oneself.

Honesty is a pure relation to Self and the own original will.

Communication that is open and honest will fully bring forth the person, nothing is hidden and no lies are created.

Love in human relations

When there is fully open and good communication between two persons, their nearness will grow. If the communication remains good, it will also improve and its level will grow. Then the growth of nearness will never stop, in other words the relation will improve constantly.

If the communication is honest, that is if both parts are fully honest to oneself and open to each other, then the growth of nearness is strong and their mutual relation will take the form it should really have. It can be friendship, but it can also be a relationship, but in any case it will be true.

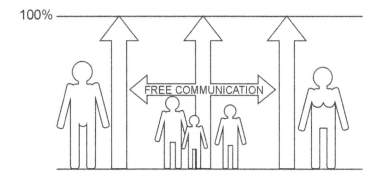

The picture presents the persons' relation to their own wills, and their mutual area's relation to their mutual purpose.

The vertical arrows on the sides illustrates the level of responsibility for the own wills of the persons that are creating a mutual area. The vertical arrow in the middle illustrates the condition of the mutual area compared to the purpose of the jointly created intention.

In the picture the communication, which is illustrated by the horizontal arrow, is honest and open, nothing is concealed. Neither one of them reduces anything of their own original wills, but takes full responsibility for their own as well as the mutual. The parts also help each other to take responsibility for their original own wills.

To the common that is born in the relationship comes a family that is balanced. Each and everyone is given as much space as possible and help for the real own will, as well as the creation of a person in accordance with it.

Friendship functions the same way, only its common doesn't create a family but is something else that is in everyone's favor.

Honesty to oneself in this context doesn't have to mean a fully reached Self, but it means that the persons are on their way to themselves and they both already have an existing conscious connection to Self. When there exists a conscious connection to Self, the person is clearly approaching it, and he won't change the direction of his path. Without this connection the person is unstable in relation to himself, or then he isn't conscious of his real self at all.

Without a connection to Self, true love doesn't exist, since true love is flow between the beings. Without this connection the person is in the lie, in the world's thought, let be that he can fulfill some degree of love like nearness and feeling of togetherness.

100% ─────────────────────────────────────

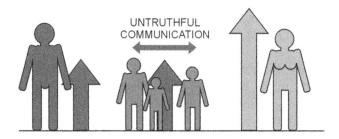

In this picture, the levels of responsibility of the persons are low and it affects the whole family. The picture illustrates the family creating parents influence on themselves, each other and their family. Other possible influences aren't taken into account here.

Untruthful communication means that it isn't honest to oneself, and that it isn't fully open. Untruthfulness isn't just conscious lying or concealing, it is also reduction of the own person, which is reduction of the own will and the consciousness. It is untruthful even if the person imagines that he is unknowing of it.

The communication of the couple isn't open. Both reduce something of their own real wills, and the level of the common is set on the level of the one who takes less responsibility for the own real level, since it can't be higher than that.

Neither of them takes full responsibility for the own original will. If one of them would, he wouldn't reduce himself and he would have to demand that the other improves the condition of the own will, or to notice that the relationship doesn't function, in other words that there isn't any.

Reducing oneself is inner dishonesty, which can be concealing or lying outwards. Concealing is to hide something of importance and lying is to tell untruths. All lying begins with inner dishonesty.

This kind of relationship can be corrected by admitting the distance that in fact exists.

The premise for correcting isn't a thought, according to which it necessarily would be a relationship. To correct is to find the real existing distance and the true character of the relation, regardless of what they are.

True love and honesty in the common space is possible only in fulfilling the own true self. It is to take responsibility for the original own will. It is not possible if not both fully takes that responsibility.

One must see that the honesty and openness in the communication really is such that the own person isn't concealed or reduced to please the other part, or for any other reason.

A person that is in the world's thought doesn't take responsibility for the own original will. Therefore he isn't, and can't be, fully open in relation to his own original will and his person. He doesn't have a connection to it.

The idea of love offered by the world's thought remains on a level of wishing, since it doesn't contain flow between the beings, but is an imaginary world that remains on the thought level. The persons won't reach love, but they can reach compatibility of thoughts.

If they both are in the world's thought and their conscious self and strive is on a thought level, they can inside the frames of the world's thought create a relationship that functions as well as they take responsibility for the persons they believe they are. It functions as long as none of them changes his mind about the person he believes to be.

If either one of them changes his mind, for example by starting to lift forth the own real will, then the situation changes. This is why relationships based on the world's thought are unstable. The own real will doesn't change, it is completely stable. It progresses, but its direction doesn't change.

Those who still have an existing connection to the own self can experience love with its true meaning within the boundaries of the clearness of the consciousness. The closer their persons are to the world's thought, the less they can experience true love.

Those who still have a quite strong connection to self, but the grip of the world's thought is also strong, are in a conflicting situation between the world's thought and the own thought. For them love can be especially painful, since they strongly experience that it exists, but that it won't be fulfilled and it can't be fulfilled.

Distances in relationships

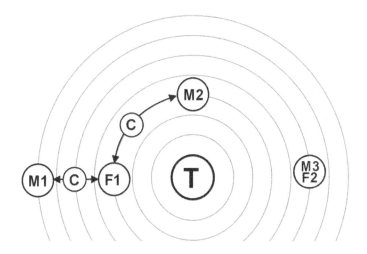

This picture illustrates the distances between the persons' mutual relation to each other and the truth.

The diagram is an aid for observation of the matter. In it, each persons' distance from the truth is the person's average distance from the truth.

The truth "T" is here equal to a person in accordance with the own original will. The more specifically the person (M or F) corresponds to Self's intention with its person in that moment, the closer the person is to the truth.

For the persons, who have some distance to each other, to be able to create something common, they must make a compromise (C). Here the compromise is a compromise between levels of truth. Then the persons have to, in their actions, apply a level of truth that differs from their own level of truth in relation to their own real person, to be able to fulfill something common.

M1 and F1 are in the lie in the same direction, but on different distances. Same direction means that their conception of the world is similar, but for M1 it's more rough, less true.

For them to be able to tie some kind of a relation between each other, they have to make a compromise. No solution is fully good to neither of them.

If the relation is a less binding one, it might serve its purpose, but the closer relationship it is in question, the more certainly it won't function.

In principal M1 could move his viewpoint closer to the truth, but approaching the truth would be difficult and it is uncertain if he wants it so much that it is done with a sufficient speed.

In this situation F1 should try to help M1 closer to the truth. If M1 doesn't approach the truth, the only right solution is that F1 doesn't do anything common that requires proximity with M1, since the more close relation they intend to have, the more F1 would have to lie to herself.

F1 could lower her level of truth by lying to herself. Accomplishing that wouldn't require a lot of time, it happens fast if F1 creates a believable explanation to herself, with which help she ties herself to M1. The explanation is a lie that is used to grow the distance from the truth.

According to that explanation it is right and necessary to do so. This is more usual than that M1 would approach the truth to reduce the distance. In this case it is usually a question of wishing for nearness and since there is none, an image of nearness is created by lying.

The wishing in these kinds of situations can be very strong, and abandoning it can even be very difficult and painful. Regardless of that, the lie doesn't make it true and F1 deceives herself with it. In fact she deceives both with that lie, since she lies about herself even to the other part.

F1's relation to M2 would as a compromise bring forth a solution, where they both would have to accept habits that differ from the ordinary modes of action for each one of them, but the level of truth of the compromise would be the same for both. Therefore there wouldn't be a lot of conflict in other than the modes of action. They could have problems with understanding each other's modes of action, even if they would be equally honest.

F2 and M3 are in the same direction and at the same distance from the truth, in which case they might create even a close relation. They have compatibility of thoughts.

When the person has a distance from the truth in relation to the own real will, then the person's condition is unstable, since he might happen to approach the truth or grow away from it and change the direction of position. If it is a question of a long-term relation and both parts change considerably, then the relation will end if the distance grows too much.

If the persons from start are sufficiently close to each other, in relation to the truth about their own persons, and both are willing to move towards the truth, the relation will function regardless of the changes, since a possible compromise would approach the truth and its functionality would grow.

Then the relation might however change its character, if the persons at start were too far away from the truth to be able to define its character correctly. While the truth grows, the character of the relation might dawn to be different than what they believed when it started. This regardless of that their nearness will grow with the growth of the truth.

Changing of the character of the relation in such cases isn't a bad thing at all. Besides, the starting character of the relation might even have served both persons approaching of the truth at that time, and then it was good for both of them at that time.

Love problems

Love problems in this context means problems in a relationship between a man and a woman, which are problems in the mutual relationship.

If even one of them isn't honest to himself, the feeling of nearness is wishing for nearness, not nearness. It might be to see a possibility of nearness, but the nearness can't be fulfilled.

Inside the frames of the world's thought there can't be real love, since the connection between the beings is missing. Without this connection a true flow doesn't exist, but only a wish for that flow.

Love stories are based on wishing for love. The human doesn't really have any other kind of love than a wish for it. Exceptions are extremely rare.

The beautiful pictures of love stories are pictures of submission, since the love they illustrate doesn't ever reach higher than that in reality. Wishing doesn't rise higher up than submission.

People's idea of love between man and woman is seen and is formed to a big extent out of love stories, which are beautiful pictures of wishing for love. People create their own ideas out of the love stories, which all are a product of the world's thought.

The world's thought is in the present world so far away from Self, the own will and the awareness of it, that its idea of love is impregnated with power game and physicality. Therefore they also contain a lot of desire to possess, lust for power and submission.

Two persons might experience arousing love, when the beings experience a momentary connection under easy circumstances, which creates a wish and makes it strong.

Their inner obstacles haven't in that moment yet been revealed, but quite instantly the contact will bring up the obstacles and some degree of distance is set between them. They might notice the obstacles, but try to pretend that they don't exist. They are dishonest to themselves and each other and they try to defeat the obstacles by pretending that they don't exist.

Unfortunately they won't disappear by pretending and therefore love is left on a level of wishing. It can't rise up to flourish since a free flow can't be formed between them.

The requirement of free flow is in inner honesty that will lead to sufficient insight of Self, and that way to the understanding of the own will. Then both of them can grow to be their own persons and their mutual flow is freed.

This must happen in both, since only the other parts approaching of Self isn't enough. On the contrary, the growth of the other person's level of truth will increase their mutual distance.

Another way to experience arousing love is to experience the other person to be a part of a self created image made by love stories and ideas, in which case the object of the feeling of love isn't really the other person, but a fantasy-image of the person. In this case the other part is expected to act according to that image, in other words the person wants the other part to play a role in accordance with the own fantasy-image. If this doesn't happen, then it is very easy to experience disappointment in the other parts behavior.

Both ways lead, if continued, to a relation that is maintained with the help of thought-images, in which the ways of acting are agreed upon for them to be able to remain together and experience some kind of mutuality. This mutuality is dependency and habit, not real connection. It can be called compatibility of thoughts.

Therefore it will gradually go flat and turn into a plain human relation, and often it leads to such a strong weakening of the relation, that they will no longer experience any connection between each other.

If they to some degree manage to bring forth their true selves into their lives, they might even experience true love, but it will be very poor compared to that they would have a conscious connection to the own will and could really be who they are.

Broken hearts

Behind broken hearts there is wishing.

There has been a relationship that was based on wishing for love. If it would have been real love, it would have been true nearness, and it wouldn't have ended.

Holding on to something by wishing doesn't change anything, but it causes pain.

In this case the producer of the pain is the person himself. He holds on to something he believes he wants or has achieved, and compares it to the current situation. Pain is born out of the distance between them.

By abandoning the wishing, he gets rid of the pain without losing anything.

First love

Especially when they are young, persons believe naively that love has been fulfilled, when they experience excitement of what they believe is reaching the other.

Besides that, they have also learned, from the world of adults, the world's thought's ideas of love and relationships. Their trust in the fulfilling of love is total, if they don't yet have a suspicion about the functionality of the ideas they have learned.

The disappointment is strong when reality shows to be very different. They aren't disappointed just because of the losing of what they believed was love, but also that the conception of the world doesn't function.

Since they have no ability to question what they have learned, they don't know what happened. They don't understand that the learned conception of the world is faulty, and they don't understand that the pain is caused by it.

They have believed in the world's thought's ideas of romantic love, which were taught by the adults. When they notice that it isn't fulfilled in the way they believed, it is a painful disappointment to them.

For some this phenomenon, which is thought to be first love, repeats itself throughout life.

Unfortunately the disappointment can lead to a condition, where the person believes himself to be flawed in some way, or useless, since he experiences to have been abandoned.

This feeling is born out of the image, that the failure was caused by himself, even though it was caused by that real reaching didn't happen, and in fact couldn't even have happened.

Relativity in life

Relativity

Relativity means that something is compared to something else, in other words the mutual relations between two or more things are being observed.

As an example we compare a football and the moon with each other. The moon is compared to the football an extremely big ball. The football is compared to the moon an extremely small ball.

If we compare the moon to the sun, the moon is an extremely small object and the sun an extremely big object.

In this example big and small are relative, in other words if something is big or small depends on what it is compared to.

In the comparison that happens in the mind something can for example be held for a good or a bad thing, depending on what it is compared to.

Relativity in the foundations of life

The person's life is built out of the thought models that he maintains.

The person's ideas of the values of life, good, bad and the truths of life are for him the correct ways to live and exist. He keeps this thought model as the model for the life he wishes, and on which he compares everything in his life. It functions as the base of comparison regardless of how true it is.

The only right base of comparison for the person's life is his own original will. To the extent his life isn't the same as the own original will in the moment of comparison, his life is untruthful.

The person's relation to the thought about the own person, which was created by Self, is the only right guidance of life.

Relativity of emotions

The feelings experienced by the person are based on comparisons, in other words relations between thoughts. The person uses a thought as a base of comparison, and he believes it to be true and to define the values of life. He compares his life to it in all its matters.

As a result of this comparison he gets himself answers, according to which something is good or bad. Being good and bad is equal to the distance from the base of comparison. The closer something is to the base of comparison, the better condition he experiences that matter to be in.

Mostly the comparison isn't conscious thinking, but it is observation that happens deeper within. There might be conscious comparing to some degree, but the result of the comparison is still influenced by many matters that aren't in the consciousness.

The comparing happens all the time. What are being compared are the conditions of all the person's matters in relation to his base of comparison of how all matters should be.

The person holds some thoughts for true and compares his understanding of life with them. The comparison tells the distance between them as the person understands it. The feeling he experiences is born out of the distance he experiences in the comparison.

The greater the distance is, the more miserable feeling he will experience. The lesser the distance is, the better he feels.

The feeling isn't based on the truth, it is based on the comparison and the result of the comparison.

The results of the comparison depend on what was compared to what. The base of comparison might be wrong and besides that, the matters that are compared to it might also be wrong.

It is important to find the right base of comparison, which is the own real will, and moreover to be able to clearly see the truth about the condition of the person oneself has created.

Since the fundamental ideas of the world's thought are in most people's minds the thoughts they make the comparison to, the feelings are very similar for most people. This is why a lot of people believe those feelings to be true in such way that if something is like this and this, then you feel like that.

Many experience people who don't compare matters the same way, and who don't get the same or as strong emotions as result, to be insensitive.

Experienced as a sensitive person is someone, who with his comparison often gets a result that tells about a very big distance and he experiences a lot of pain.

Forming of the base of comparison

People mostly use the world's thought in the comparison, since they have been brought up to it, and therefore they also look for solutions to life in binding to the world's thought. One gets a lot of support when binding to that thought, since people around one support the binding to it.

There is no support for the own thought, and its existence isn't even confirmed. Therefore it comes in second when choosing the base of comparison. For many people it is preserved in the consciousness to some extent until youth, but they can't manage to get it to be dominant. The own thought gradually fades away and the world's thought is formed to be the only base of comparison, whereby one's own person is no longer affected by one's own thought at all.

For some a connection to the own thought is preserved throughout life even as a strong source of influence on the base of comparison, but its effect remains as anxiety that won't leave them alone since they don't know what it is, they only feel its existence.

To the extent the person has an existing connection to himself, to the extent its effect is included in the comparison. If the person strives towards the right defined by the world's thought, then he strives away from his own will. Then the distance to the own thought grows and the distance to the world's thought decreases, in which case he feels relief in relation to the world's thought and pain in relation to the own thought.

Since there is support for the world's thought, it is strong and since there is no support for the own thought, it remains weak. If the person manages to reveal the lie of the world's thought, its grip weakens and the strength of the own will grows. Correspondingly, if the person forgets his own thought, the strength of the world's thought grows and the influence of the own thought gets weaker.

To achieve a completely painless feeling, one of them has to step aside completely. The person has to either forget himself completely and create his person in accordance with the world's thought in a way where it is not influenced by anything else than the world's thought.

The instances that represent the world's thought support the adapting to the world's thought and the forgetting of Self. Their premise is that the world's thought is true and that it is the ideal.

For the person's own thought, Self, the own will, there hardly is any space in this world. Very few instances are kind enough to even give it space to exist. Getting support and help for growing up to be your own self is even harder to get.

The distance between the world's thought and the own thought is very big in the present world.

The own will

There is only one true will

The true own will rises from Self.

The own will is created by Self, and the person has had it since birth. It is a will that defines the whole essence of the person's life and its goals.

The own will isn't unrighteous, selfish, uncaring, lazy or negative in any way.

The own will is always good.

The own will never violates others own wills, but instead it supports also their fulfillment.

The own will is the person's purpose of life.

The own will's relation to life

Before the beginning of life Self is without a body, in other words it is not a part of life in that moment. It creates a thought about joining life and then it also creates a thought about what it wants to do in life.

The definition of doing is some accomplishment that has a result defined by the will.

Nobody is born to do nothing.

The own will's position in life is very central and it has to be fully dominant. The purpose of the person's life is in it, and he has no reason to join any other thought or to abandon his own will.

The own will is the person's only reason to live.

The world we want is the sum of everyone's own wills.

The own will's problematical relation to the world

The world of the present man is very much controlled by the thought of entertainment and making money in a way where money gives a direction to life. With money one gets a safe position in the power game and satisfaction is sought in entertainment, which is an attempt to replace the inner satisfaction that is born out of the fulfilling of the original own will.

Money very often functions as a tool to control the person's work effort. When the person gives his work effort to goals defined by the world's thought, he gets money for it, and with that money he can build a life that he imagines to want.

This way the persons focus is shifted from the fact, that he doesn't use his work effort to fulfill his own real will. Even his wage he usually uses on things that are valued by the world's thought. Hence, both his work effort and his wage serves something else than the fulfilling of his real will.

The human has been taught that he needs to do work with something that someone else defines and pays wage for, and the wage is in turn used to entertainment and the frameworks of the personal life. The person's own real will can't be seen anywhere in this structure.

The blame for the controlling influence of money can't be put on the money, since money is nothing but a tool. The controlling influence is born out of peoples own ways of thinking and making choices. Money will in one form or another be a means of exchange even in the free world, but there it won't be the factor that controls people's life choices as it very much is in the present world.

If someone has some kind of a memory and will of something own, then the strive is to direct it into being a hobby, which one can do if there happens to be time from the things that the world's thought defines as important.

The world's thought favors bypassing of the own will and the bowing under the power of others, which is submission to others thoughts and abandonment of the own thought.

A world that respects and favors the own will is the world that everybody ultimately wants. Still hardly anyone tries even the least to fulfill it.

The unwillingness to fulfill the world that was originally intended is caused by that people have submitted to the thoughts of persons who desire power. The power system has very thoroughly gained control over everything, and because of that, submission to it is for most people even the prerequisite to stay alive.

The system in power creates the conditions for life, and to deviate from them can produce problems. Depending on the country, deviation from the conditions set by the power is always problematic, and might even be life threatening.

The power system determines the goals and the needs. It raises people to accept the power system as a natural state. It educates people for its own good and it determines the valuations. The power systems control people's lives quite completely, even if it is a question of a democracy.

The grip of the hierarchical power is so utterly complete, that it controls even the culture and art, which also are built on its principals. Power supports culture that supports the existence of power and acknowledges its principals.

Its influence isn't shaken by election results or revolutions as long as people believe in the necessity and naturalness of the power system. The system has been grown into people's thoughts, and therefore it is complete power. Inside the small frames set by it one can experience freedom, which even that is seeming freedom.

Many have tried to change the power system into a better one, but it has happened inside the frames of the power system. Seen from the viewpoint of human freedom, such a change is as best only to ease the pain, not solving of the actual problem.

The fundamental problem is the binding of people under the rule of outer power. That problem hasn't been tried to remove, and it won't be tried until people are willing enough to take responsibility for their own wills, their own selves and the purposes of their lives. This requires a strong growth of consciousness among mankind.

The world of the free will

The free will mustn't be tied to anything by others.

The person creates his ties himself in accordance with his own will, in which case he can of his free will choose to help something that he values. He has no reason to value anything else more than that.

The free world is born out of people's own wills. It is the sum of everyone's own wills.

When the thought of the free world is pondered over, a question of how it could be fulfilled easily arises. Usually the questioners thinking is based on the models of the power system, according to which someone has to control this freedom and create a system for its fulfilling, and give a permission to it.

Thinking like this the premise would just be another form of the power system, in which case the power system would remain in control.

When we think about a really free world, which is based on the sum of the free wills, we can't do much more than state, that it is up to them who somewhere in the future fulfills it. We in this time have no reason to ponder over it, and those in the future won't need our advice.

They know what they are doing, we don't know what they are doing and what they should do. We don't even have to know. Our objective is to change the world so that the future gets a chance. The future will take care of itself.

Freedom of the own will

The motion of life

The motion of life means the direction of life, and the velocity the person's life is progressing with.

This motion is influenced by the person's inner condition, the outer thoughts that influences it, the person's own interpretations of them and the person's own original will on the level of consciousness, on which he has it.

This motion is free, when its steering force is the own will's thought.

Free motion is a right given by nature. Each and everyone is born free.

Freedom

Freedom is motion of the original own will.

Freedom is a right given by nature and it regards every human.

Depriving of freedom is to subject another person's own will to an outer thought.

Depriving and restricting freedom is always wrong.

Prisoner of thought

A person whose life's most significant motion setting force is some outer thought isn't free, but is instead a prisoner of that outer thought.

He might think he is free, but by observing the matter more closely he can notice, that he as a definition of freedom uses the controlling outer thought's idea of freedom. It is not difficult to guess, that the outer thought doesn't define itself to be a depriver of freedom.

The existing societies raise their children to be prisoners of the society's thought models. This happens in the upbringing and in the schools.

Its most significant influence on children is born out of that the members of society are generally agreed about the so called right ways to think. The fundamental self-evident idea is holding the hierarchical power system as true. It effectively removes the own will from being a life steering and dominating factor.

The depriving of freedom is very commonly called morally right, for the society's best, liberation, helping, thinking about the person's own good or anything else with which the person can be made to believe that it is good for him and that it is right.

Even if the person doesn't hold it for good and right, the subjugator still experiences that he has a great motive and justification for this subjecting. Then the subjugator experiences that he means good and therefore that he is right.

This kind of subjecting is the most usual one. It happens unconsciously, and the person can't even experience to be a subjugator, since the environment supports him and it often is thought of as goodness.

Sometimes the subjugator is aware of that there is no justification, and the motives for depriving freedom are conscious lies, but then it is a question of a person who is very greedy for power, and who believes in his right to control others.

Neither one of these types of subjugators really believes in their justifications, but their consciousness is very weak. For them the approaching of Self and the reaching of the own will's freedom can be very difficult.

Their condition is caused by a weak ability to confront, in other words they haven't managed to solve their inner problem and free the own will. They have a lot of fears concerning themselves that prevent them, and they might try to hide from themselves by fleeing into materialism.

Fleeing into materialism is an attempt to convince oneself that the fundamental reasons of life are material and that the body's importance is central for selfhood, and also overvaluation of material pleasures.

It is fleeing into materialism, since it is distancing from Self. It is movement towards the absolute lie, in other words transformation into matter. The person chooses to decrease his consciousness instead of growing it. He reduces himself instead of starting to take responsibility for his own person.

To raise the body's importance to be central when defining selfhood leads to the decreasing of consciousness, where the survival of the body level is a central matter, and a significant part of it is the acquisition of power. Then the level of consciousness has strongly approached the level of the animal, which is what the body ultimately is.

Fleeing into materialism is at worst to be on the animal level of consciousness as a leader animal, or to be subjected to its power and be content with that.

Both the subjugator and the subjected flee into materialism for the same reason. Neither of them dares to begin approaching themselves, since they experience fear. They create their persons into being a leader animal and a humble servant of the leader animal.

With their thoughts they support the justification of power and the subjecting of others. Their relation to Self is very distant and therefore they enjoy life seeking for material pleasure.

Those who most strongly flee into materialism support a strong leader and enjoy the assembly, regardless of which position in the power hierarchy they are in.

There are other reasons to support a strong leader. The most usual reason is despair in the disorder of society, which usually is caused by those in animal consciousness, who were previously mentioned. Then the person, in his opinion, chooses the lesser evil.

Free motion and the loss of it

When he is born the person has a free own will, that Self has defined already before the birth.

Then the idea of his own will is the quintessential idea of his life. It contains everything about the purpose of his life and it defines the wanted direction of life for the one who is born.

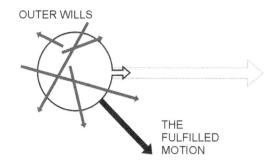

OUTER WILLS

THE
FULFILLED
MOTION

Instantly after birth he starts to get influenced by the ideas of life, the purpose of life and the valuations of life that are offered by the environment. These differ from the person's own will's thought, and the many ideas of life that are offered, are on top of all contradictory with each other.

The child's problem in this situation is that he can't do anything else but to copy everything and that way create a viewpoint for life in accordance to the environment, and that will be the starting viewpoint of his life.

This copying is necessary for him, since in other case there wouldn't develop any viewpoint for life, in which case he isn't a part of life. He would remain very distant of the surrounding world.

At first the child doesn't evaluate the quality of the guiding to life at all. At the beginning he copies everything such as it is offered, but step by step he starts to choose what he copies.

The child might even at a very early stage experience that the offered information and his own will are contradictory, and it might lead to some degree of isolation from life.

The strength of his awareness of the own will and the importance of the intended life's cause has an influence on this shielding, which can cause isolation from other humans. A strongly isolated easily creates his own separate worlds, and he doesn't experience nearness to the world, which idea he can't experience to identify with, without at the same time losing his own.

An own separate world isn't more unreal than the reality, that is commonly accepted. It is different and there are fewer members in that world. Its contact surface to the reality experienced by other people is smaller than usual. We have to remember, that worlds are born out of joint realities, shared ideas of life.

In fact there are as many worlds as there are people, if we are precise, since the same world is only the part that is shared reality, in other words what we have the same idea of.

In the free world of own wills the mutual relations would be considerably much stronger, and therefore the shared we experience would be much wider and stronger.

Other people might think that the one who isolates himself is less social, but he is not, since one who protects the idea of the own will is all else but unsocial. He is trying to save his purpose.

He doesn't necessarily succeed with that very well, since he can't find a way for that purpose to be fulfilled. He might be trapped in his own isolation, and irresolute in relation to it. If he manages to find even a few small gaps, through which he can fulfill his actual will, then he will do that.

When this is compared with the impact caused by the lives of those who have abandoned their own wills, then this impact on the world is a lot better than the damage that the ones who have abandoned their wills caused themselves, others and the coming generations.

However, this shouldn't be understood so that the person in this finds a justification for his isolation, or a discharge from responsibility for freeing the own will.

The growth of the distance from the own will

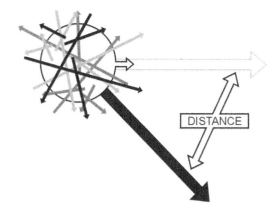

As life progresses, the child copies more instructions for life from his environment. Since the instructions in the present world doesn't include any information about the real own will, the real own will can't manage to form in the person's mind as the life dominant factor.

Because of this the fulfilled life progresses in a different direction than the wanted life. To the extent the person is aware of what occurs, it makes him anxious. The amount of pain is equal to the distance he is aware of.

Pain in general is the difference between any wished state and prevailing state. The pain spoken of here is associated with consciousness of the difference between the motion defined by the own will and the fulfilled motion. As a pain it lies very deep within, and it can't be removed in any other way than by reducing the distance to the life meant by the own will.

The pain can be removed from consciousness by forgetting, in other words by lowering the consciousness, which means abandoning oneself. However, it won't disappear but is in unconsciousness waiting for the time when the person strives towards inner freedom.

The motion of human life is determined by the thoughts offered in the upbringing and the education. For some, the own will influences it to some extent, but usually its strength is too weak for its influence to be significant.

The person's life controlling thought model is therefore formed of a selection of outer thoughts, which the person believes to be his own. His part in it is nonetheless only the choosing of the offered alternatives.

Freedom to choose from offered alternatives is often thought of as freedom and freedom of choice. In reality it is a very limited freedom of choice, since choosing outside of the offered alternatives is prevented.

Prevention of other alternatives are for example arguments like that doesn't exist, you can't do like that, that isn't needed and so on.

Regardless of the motive for the delimiting, it is an effort to silence the own real will, since it is not compatible with the fundamental ideas of the hierarchical world power.

The thoughts offered by the world are thoughts built on the idea of the hierarchical power system. Therefore there is nothing in those thoughts that supports the own original will, only such that discriminate it.

Returning to the own will's route

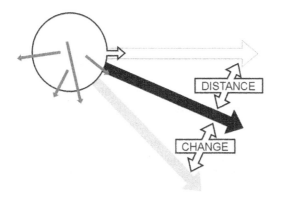

The route to the life defined by the own will goes through the revealing of lies. As the person manages to see through the lies, which he has collected in his mind, their force disappears. They cease to influence.

The own will is therefore not found by studying the own will, or by searching for it, but by freeing it. It hasn't been lost anywhere besides underneath the lies. Therefore the return is dissolution of lies, in which case the free will comes forth by itself when the lies are cleared away.

The truth is an imperishable thing, and so is the own will. When revealing lies, only lies disappear. If the person by mistake holds for a lie, and believes to have revealed a lie, something that is true, it won't disappear, but will at some point come back. It can stay hidden for some time, since defining something as a lie with wrong motives is itself a lie that covers the truth.

One doesn't have to be worried about losing the own will, or the truth, since they don't disappear by any means.

As the lies disappear and cease to influence, the person's

consciousness of his own self is freed. The amount of pain decreases as the conscious distance decreases.

One must notice, that the consciousness of the distance might grow during this time, since full consciousness of the distance has been reached only when the consciousness has reached the own will. Then the amount of pain also grows. This doesn't mean that the person's condition has worsened, rather it has improved, even if the pain momentarily is stronger.

When the freeing of the own will progresses, its motion grows. When it has been reached to some extent, it will immediately start to influence. At first the error is big, but if the person continually reduces the lies, the error decreases. One must not be afraid of the error, or care about it. It can't be allowed to stop the motion of life, except if it is of harm to oneself or others.

Fear of pain

Many people who seek for inner freedom believe that inner freedom is to be found in the direction of painlessness. In that case they are seeking for harmony, in other words painless states, instead of the truth.

If the goal is inner harmony, then the confrontation of lies is avoided. The easiest route to harmony is to lower the consciousness so that the awkward truth, that reminds one of the lies, ceases to effect. On this route that aims to harmony one is very commonly lost in a beautiful image of the truth, which is created by imagination and isn't true at all.

Reaching the truth isn't painless and the one seeking it can't fear pain. It is a route that contains pain and fear, and he who gives in to them will never reach the truth, since he is not willing to confront the lies that cause the pain.

On that route inner harmony will come as a consequence of the opening of the consciousness, since the force of the lies weakens and the person's conflict in relation to his own self decreases. It is the only real and lasting harmony.

Decrease of the distance

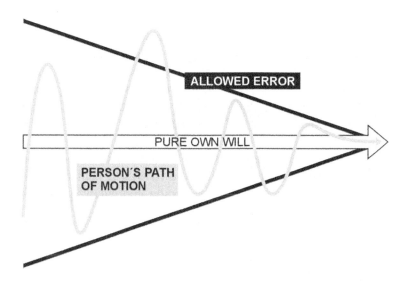

In the middle of the picture there is a white arrow that illustrates the own will's accurate path of motion. The black line illustrates the allowed error, which decreases in relation to the own will's accurate path of motion in time. The gray curving line illustrates the person's path of motion, which is the fulfilling of life in time.

It is impossible to reach the pure own will immediately when one starts focusing on solving the problem with selfhood and the own will.

Self isn't an unrealistic daydreamer, but rather a very patient and resolute guide for its own person. We might say that it is a question of an exceptionally good self-upbringing. This is however restricted by the person's willingness to really hear himself.

When the person starts approaching his own will, he has an allowed error set by himself. The boundaries of the error are defined so that the magnitude of the error doesn't prevent or slow down the approaching of the own will.

In the picture, the path of motion exceeds the allowed error a few times and at those points the person feels pain to the extent he is honest to himself. He knows that the error is too great, but he could also close his eyes from it to protect the self-deception. If he returns inside of the allowed error, then he is again approaching his own will and the understanding of it.

Staying inside the boundaries of the allowed error is for the one who approaches oneself equal to the own will. It is that with the best possible accuracy, and if the person continually grows the accuracy, Self experiences the situation as good.

At some point the person reaches his own will and is fully conscious of it. He is fully in it and fully capable of remaining in it.

The danger of bindings

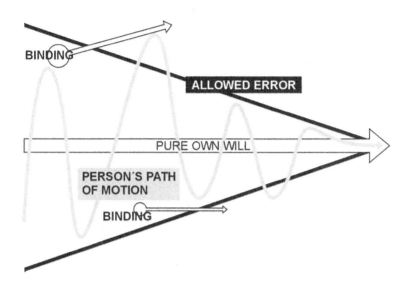

If one makes bindings in life that oblige for a long period of time, the bindings might at the time of their creation feel like they fit inside the error of the own will. Then the person doesn't at that moment experience the disadvantage they bring later on.

The picture illustrates bindings, which direction in development aren't beneficial for the freeing of the own will in the long term. Their direction deviates from the direction that is a prerequisite for the freeing of the own will.

At some point their influence on the person's motion takes him outside the allowed error line for the progress of the own will. In this case the person needs to correct the situation by any means necessary. In other case he jeopardizes his whole liberation.

Long term bindings shouldn't be made before the own will's path of motion is accurate enough, and the person's ability to evaluate the direction of the bindings is good enough.

If the binding is a human relation, then the binding has to be evaluated honestly by looking into if the person in question is on the path of the own will. If he is not, or if he is that weakly compared to the own path of motion, then the binding will be a burden. It actually is a burden already in that moment, since it pulls towards the outer line of the allowed error from start. In other words, it doesn't at any point serve the approaching of the own will's path of motion.

If one thinks oneself to be able to help the other part of the human relation to change his path of motion, so that it moves towards the own will's path of motion at a sufficient speed compared to one's own, then the binding's path of motion shouldn't be evaluated as anything else besides what has already been fulfilled. What is imagined or wished for isn't true.

In that kind of helping one must be sure to notice that the person's real path of motion is what it is with his own strength. When influencing the person's path of motion with inspiration, pressure or in any other way, it doesn't rise from his own strength, and therefore it isn't his actual path of motion in a reliable way.

Even on the path that strives towards freedom, people quite easily accept errors that influence their path of motion until it leads to chaos. The reason is the low level of responsibility.

One doesn't want to tackle some problem, even if it would be possible to see long before it becomes a problem. When the problem is addressed, it has already caused a lot of damage and solving it might be so difficult, that many submits to it, and in the end never solves it.

A significant factor when approaching the own will is to be on the alert considering the own bindings, so that one doesn't make bindings without knowing the duration of the effect they have. And when making a binding to check, in a way honest to oneself and without wishful images, what the direction of the binding is during the time of its influence.

One must notice that not any wishes can change the facts. The required direction set by some binding is what it is. Lying to oneself about it would be self-deception.

Thought models also function like the mentioned bindings. They are bindings that influence the own will's direction, and the origin of those bindings are the ways to handle matters offered by some other persons. They have been offered either directly or indirectly in such way, that the person based on them has built something that looks like something own. However, their origin is not the own will.

If the person isn't willing to abandon some ways of thinking, he himself maintains the bindings that complicate his route to reach the free will.

Behind the bindings made with contracts are also the ways of thinking, and by observing that way they are also products of the ways of thinking. To disassemble bindings that are made with contracts it isn't enough to just change the way of thinking. Therefore changing them is more difficult. First one must change the way of thinking and after that also the contracts made with the environment.

The own person and the artificial person

The own person

The own person is a product of Self, the artificial person is a product of others.

Self creates a will that is meant to be the dominant thought in the person it creates. When it succeeds, it has an own person.

The idea that Self created about the own person, its aim in life and the goals, exists already before birth. It is the person's only purpose. It is his purpose of life, and his only responsibility. All other responsibilities are invented by others and they have been indoctrinated into the person's mind with lies, so that the person can be made a part of the centralistic world's thought and made to abandon himself.

The own person is the fulfillment of Self's thought, which success is the only thing that brings true satisfaction in the person's life. The own original will is always good, and it contains all the parts of the person's own world. It is not selfish in a way where the person would be self-centered, and without any regard to others.

His will contains everything about his life, starting with what he wants to accomplish during his lifetime. It also contains an idea of how his own family will be, how he is as a person and so on. It is an all covering, all viewpoints including, perfect thought that is planned concerning every detail to serve his purpose.

The higher level of requirements the person's purpose has, the more accurate and detailed his will is in relation to his life. The person's participation in life can contain quite many options, if his purpose is fulfilled within the frames of several alternatives. If the fulfilling of his will requires accuracy in human relations as well as other matters, then the plan of his life is more detailed and can cover exact definitions also for the human relations.

The person's values are tied to Self's viewpoint, in other words with its purposes. That which serves the deepening of the spiritual truth in the own person and other persons, is good and valued. As an opposite are the things that lead towards the artificial person, and all that isolates one from the truth, they are not good and valued.

Wealth is for the own person a means to achieve goals, not the purpose itself. He strives to create wealth to serve the goals of his own will. If wealth isn't required, he won't be motivated in creating wealth, since focusing on that would be a waste of time in relation to the purpose.

For the own person the leading thought of the own life is the by Self created idea of the creation. Self is the one who creates. In other words, the own person is a creation, which fundamental thought is created by Self.

The own person's relation to other persons is determined by a mutual thought, whose part every own person is. This mutual thought is an agreement of activities made between the beings. The entirety is then lead by the mutual thought of the beings, which has been created before the birth of the partakers. The leading thought forms in the material world as groups, who create mutual bindings for the activity according to the original plan.

This group thought is a cohesive force, which success also means the success of the own thoughts of the group members. Activity without hierarchical power isn't random anarchy, but very well organized activity that is agreed upon between free wills.

In Alkuajatus writings the own person means, depending on the context, either specifically the own will's person, or the person that Self has at its disposal such as it is in that moment.

The artificial person

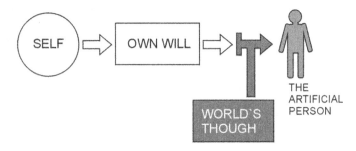

When the world's thought, in other words the fundamental thought for life that is defined by the hierarchical power and offered by the environment, influences the development of the person being created, the artificial person is born, which is a person changed by lies.

The artificial person is a product of the world's thought, and it is produced with the thoughts and valuations that the environment experiences to be correct.

These thoughts are mostly created for the needs of the centralistic thought. They are believed to be the right information about life, but they are only the right information about the centralistic thought, in other words they are thoughts of the hierarchical power's viewpoint and valuations that support it. They can also be thoughts that deviate from it or oppose it, but even those are tied to it.

The artificial person gets his satisfaction from very material things and the support from the environment, who gives its appreciation to things that serve the centralistic thought.

Fulfillers of the hierarchical thought are all who participate in it. There are those with more power, and those with less power, but they are all contributing to the fulfillment of the centralistic thought's existence, which contains the full scale of hierarchical power.

The meter of success in the artificial person's world is the success on hierarchical levels, where success grows power. Power isn't always very visible decision-making power, it is also power granted by money, in other words a relative position in wealth, which is a form of decision-making power.

In that world, the primary strive of the humans is to reach privileges for self-centered purposes. For example consumption, the acquisition of wealth and its preservation, and the appreciation offered by the world's thought are for him very central matters, and other matters are secondary.

Since this world at this time has a very strong hierarchical power system, the children are systematically raised to be parts of this world ruling thought. Then the own thoughts of the children don't get any support, but it is at best left to be a weak wish, and for most people it disappears completely while they grow up, and step by step forgets themselves and change into pure artificial persons. This usually happens at the age between18-25. This definition of age is very flexible, and there is no clear point where it happens. For some people the connection to Self remains throughout life, for most people it disappears quite early and for a few people it disappears very early.

Losing the connection is unreal in the sense that the connection to self can't be lost permanently. It always exists, since no one can seize to be his own self, even if Self is covered with so many lies that it seizes to influence life. In this context disappearing means specifically the seizing of this influence.

The return from a pure artificial person to the own person is very unlikely, but possible. In that case the person has to start seeking for his own person from a condition where he has no relation to his own person. The own person is no longer an existing thing in his consciousness. In the coming diagram his condition relative to the own person is shown as "unconsciousness".

In fact, it is almost impossible that someone is completely an artificial person that essentially is a robot controlled by thoughts, and not really even a person.

The stronger someone is an artificial person, the greater is the possibility that he is a manifestation of hunger for power, who without grief destroys anything if it serves the growth of his power. This is because it is his most central valuation, and which exceeds everything else. He might be intelligent in using the existing thoughts about fulfilling life, but he is not creative. Creativity requires at least some degree of contact to Self.

Material and spiritual values

Material and spiritual values are relative, since the materiality and the spirituality of each value depend on the level of consciousness of the person in question.

Material values are those that are based on a level of truth that is lower than the level of consciousness of the person's own original will.

Material values for each person are those that decrease the fulfilling of his own original will, and that tie him to lower levels of consciousness.

Spiritual values are those that are based on the level of truth on the person's own original will's level of consciousness.

For each person the spiritual values are the values that rise from the inner world and that raise him towards the fulfilling of his own real selfhood.

The values of the present world's thought are particularly material, since they as thoughts are values that weaken the real selfhood of the persons.

Regardless of whether the person is fulfilling material or more spiritual values, he seeks pleasure in material as well as spiritual things. The material manifestation of something doesn't make it material as a value. It is a material value to the person, if it keeps him tied to lower levels of consciousness.

The material essence of the existence is also relative. We are in any event in a material world, which whole existence is material. Thoughts are material as well as wooden statues. Their material essence is only recognized on different levels.

The lightest possible material essence is very near the absolute truth and the heaviest possible is in a state, where the consciousness falls to the level of unconscious matter.

The fundamental essence of matter is the lie. It is a lowered level of consciousness that enables the experience of existence. Motion on levels of consciousness is motion on material levels.
In practice however, when we speak of the material we usually

mean what we experience as material, the physically touchable matter that corresponds with the material level of our bodies.

Relations of the own person and the artificial person

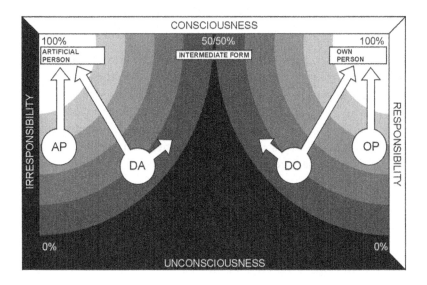

The tones in this diagram go from black to white. The black represents unconsciousness and the white consciousness in relation to something. On the left side the person is closer to the artificial person and on the right he is closer to the own person. In this context "to be something/somewhere" means the viewpoint from where the person creates his life.

On the left side is "irresponsibility" and on the right "responsibility". In this context responsibility is fulfilling the own person, in other words the person is fulfilling the world that everyone actually wants, regardless of they are aware of it or not.

Irresponsibility means the fulfilling of the hierarchical world, which is against the original own will.

The person's condition in the diagram is the person's average condition compared to the own thought and the world's thought. Different matters in the person are at different points in relation to the own person and the artificial person, but in this diagram an average condition is used to illustrate an average position.

The positions of the persons are circles that are marked with the combination of letters "AP", "DA", "DO", "OP". The arrows in the circles illustrates the directions of strive.

AP is a person who has become fully artificial, but is not fully aware of everything when it comes to the thought that is his life-controlling thought. However, only the artificial person feels real to him, and neither does he strive to any other direction. The person's set of values is therefore very material. The person's route to the own person goes through unconsciousness. In this context unconsciousness isn't loss of consciousness, but it illustrates the person's relation to something, which in this case means that in the artificial person's life-controlling thought there isn't any thought about the own person.

DA is a person who is artificially weighted and his strive is weighted towards reaching the artificial person, but the own person hasn't been fully forgotten, it is in some degree still in the mind. DA is quite far from the artificial person, but even further away from the own person, and therefore the artificial person feels more real to him, even if it is unclear. His life is confused and his condition is unbalanced. He seeks a solution for reaching balance in the artificial person.

DO is a person who is on the own person's side, but so far away that there still exists a small attraction towards the artificial person. The DO's position is quite far from the perceiving of the own person, in the diagram the gray is deep. He has a lot of unclearness regarding what he wants. He experiences a strong attraction towards the own person, but he doesn't know what it is. He has a lot of unclearness and therefore his life is unbalanced. He tries to find a solution in the direction of the own person.

OP is clearly conscious of the own person and is with determination advancing toward it. His consciousness of the own person isn't clear, but he is approaching it. He is quite balanced, even if he still is unconscious about many things. The balance is brought by a clear touch to the own person, who functions as a calm central point in life.

The lives of persons that are in an intermediate form are controlled by the thought of both sides. They have no peace, but they might create things from the own person's viewpoint. Creative work in the intermediate form is heavy and it can be painful. In other words he might be creative, even if his life-controlling thought is the artificial person. He might experience himself to be like two persons, since his life-controlling thought is divided in a way where neither side is clearly dominant. On the inside the person is in a very confused condition. Life for him is a struggle he can't solve, since both sides are equally strong.

He would be able to solve his condition by abandoning one of the two, but can't very easily find a direction. His consciousness of the own person is weak, but enough for him not to want to abandon it. The world's thought that binds him contains things which keep him tied.

What isn't presented in the diagram, are the levels of responsibility. The person's condition is in the diagram on the level of responsibility, from where he observes his life. If the level of responsibility is lowered, his experienced condition in relation to the own person is improved. If the level of responsibility is raised, his experienced condition in relation to the own person is weakened.

The level of responsibility can be made lighter by lying to oneself, but if one really intends to reach the own person, the level of responsibility must be set according to how Self has defined it, since otherwise the fulfilling of the own person isn't possible.

Lying to oneself about the level of responsibility can be very tempting. The person can experience his condition to have improved if he lowers the level. It happens so that he lowers his responsibility and imagines it to be real. Someone might lie to himself that the level of responsibility is higher than it is, by in his thought-images creating a picture of mightiness, which however is based on a thought of mightiness in accordance with the artificial person's world.

In fact, the level of responsibility can't be changed, in other words the bar can't be raised or lowered. The person has to take precisely the responsibility for his own person that it requires. The person has been planned to fulfill some specific task, and the own person has to be fulfilled accordingly.

In the diagram it is a question of life steering viewpoints, of what thoughts and valuations are controlling in the person's activities. The two sides of the diagram, the inner reality and the world's thought, are two different worlds, since especially in the present world they are to a large extent dominated by virtually opposite values.

The persons are in different viewpoints, in different inner worlds, but in the same world when we speak of the world that is fulfilled.

To one who is in the own person it is fully possible to see both worlds and to understand them completely, but his life is controlled only by the own person's world.

The artificial person in the diagram, in other words a person who is in the world's thought, is presented as a level of consciousness in relation to the world's thought. If we speak of consciousness in its actual sense, a person who is created according to the world's thought isn't conscious at all. Regarding the artificial person in the diagram it is a question of the person's relation to the world's thought, not his relation to the truth.

The artificial person isn't capable of understanding the own person's world. He might learn to understand behavior in his own person, but he can never understand the real reasons, since the understanding of those requires an inner connection to Self. To understand the artificial person's world is for him to learn to understand a learnable thought from the viewpoint of that thought.

The artificial person doesn't like those who are in the own person's world, since they don't want to build the world in accordance with the hierarchical power system, they want to build a world that isn't controlled by power, but by voluntariness.

The artificial person experiences it as a threat to his own world and classifies the own will's persons as dangerous, since they don't support his position. It is true in a way, since advantages and positions based on power disappear, if the free will comes in place.

It is in place to mention, that the diagram is meant to be a help for the understanding of different conditions, not for defining certain types of persons. People are different and there are as many types as there are people, therefore they can't be categorized with specifically named definitions.

Disorders of the mind

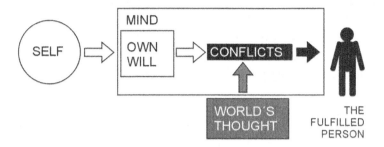

Self never has a disorder of the mind. Self doesn't have a mind. Self creates and maintains a mind. The mind is a part of the creation, in other words the viewpoint of the lowered consciousness. Therefore Self is always capable of correcting the mind, and it can't even be done by someone else.

The mind gets disturbed only by lies that confuse the person. The purpose of lies is to disturb the mind, so that the person can't be in control of himself, or in accordance to the own will.

All disorders of the mind are corrected through the revealing of lies. The person himself has to reveal a lie in his mind to himself, for the lie to stop having an influence. The lie stops having an influence on the depth where it has been revealed. Even a smaller self-conducted insight about the lie improves the person's condition to some extent.

One must notice that what heals is insight, real understanding, not accepting something as true, or its consequent understanding. Insight in this context means seeing it in the own mind and revealing the seen as a lie. Revealing it by thinking isn't enough, it has to be seeing, only then it is an insight.

Disturbances of the mind are never caused by material reasons. It is always a question of conflicts inside the mind. Efforts to correct disturbances of the mind on the material level, with medicine or by any other means on the material level, doesn't correct the error, with those the error is only prevented from being visible, and at the same time they also prevent the correction of the error. The phenomena seen in the body are only consequences, not reasons.

Mental illness doesn't exist in such a way that it would be a phenomenon comparable to a disease. Alkuajatus doesn't speak of mental disorder or mental illness, since it is not a question of a condition of sickness, as defined by the instances that help towards the world's thought, but the normal functioning of the mind. When there are conflicting thoughts in the mind, they cause problems in accordance with their strength. That is how the mind functions, and the mind isn't sick when it functions in its natural way.

The mind is however disturbed, since its strive to function in the wanted way doesn't get fulfilled, but it can't be called a sickness. Neither can this disturbance be corrected in any other way, but by revealing the lies and that way calm the activity of the mind, so that it gets balanced.

A raging person, whose mind is in a disturbed condition, is in a strong state of fear and despair. He is from a level of submission strongly aware of the distance to the own will and tries to break through to the level of anger, and that way to the level of confrontation. He isn't capable of rising to the level of confrontation, since his burden as a whole is great and he lacks information that he can use to clear his mind.

What is raging is the despair of thoughts and the desire to solve the problem. It is not the raging of the own will, or the raging of Self.

If we observe the matter more wide, then any condition where the pure fulfilling of the own will is prevented is a disturbed condition of the mind, it is only a question of the acknowledged distance. Experienced as disturbance are only conditions, where the person has problems with fulfilling his life in a way that is acceptably balanced on some level.

The disturbed condition of the person's mind doesn't tell us anything about what level of truth his own will is on. Neither does it tell us anything about how far away he is from his own will compared to other people's distances from their own wills. It only tells us about the relation between his experience of the wanted condition and his experience of the prevailing condition.

Many very capable persons suffer of disturbed conditions of the mind, since they are aware of wider and deeper areas than persons who have devoted their lives to the ordinary.

One who lives with severely disturbed conditions of the mind might keep the situation under control, if he has a lot of will power. He suffers because of it, but he is still capable of performing life and even of creating fine things, and of being a great resource to mankind.

Freedom and independence

Freedom and independence

Freedom means freedom of motion in the direction of the own original will.

Independence is solely and exclusively the own original will's dominance.

The person is independent to the extent his life choices are controlled by his real own will, and he is free to the extent he has reached the own will's freedom of motion.

The illusion of freedom and independence

The illusion of freedom is created by a feeling of freedom of motion in some direction, that isn't the direction of the own will.

The illusion of independence is the artificial person's and the environment's dominance when making choices.

Influencing factors

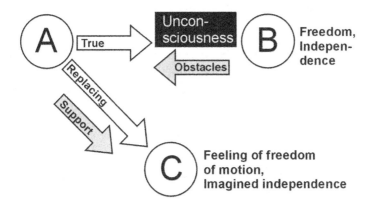

The person is at point A and his original will strives towards point B. In between are preventing forces that consist of different degrees of unconsciousness, and a pressure that is created by the environment and that resists the striving.

Unconsciousness is limitation of the consciousness. To overcome that, one must raise the consciousness so that the person's consciousness of the own will grows.

The obstacles that prevent the movement to point B are the direct and indirect resistance of the people in the environment. The world's thought doesn't support the own will's direction and the person can experience the lack of support as an indirectly influencing obstacle. Moreover, the set of values of the world's thought can resist the goal and what needs to be done to achieve the goal.

The movement towards point B is the only direction of true freedom of motion, and the only right direction of an independent person, since it is the only direction that is in the original own will's direction.

Point C is a replacing direction that the world's thought favors and supports strongly. It is a direction that strengthens the artificial person, and in that direction a diverse variety of freedom of motion is offered, encouraged by outer support.

The direction towards point C is a non-independent person's choice, where the direction isn't defined by the original own will, but by outer temptations. There exists a strong support for that direction from the world's thought, and the people who live in the world's thought favor it.

Freedom of motion is offered in that direction, but its real character is something completely different. It is a stray path, which is the artificial person's imagined will and independence, and also imagined freedom and lie that strengthens the artificial person.

Seen from the viewpoint of Self and the own original will, it is a trap that is easy to walk in to, but it leads in a direction that grows the distance to Self and the own will. It reduces freedom, even if the feeling of freedom of motion in it might offer a good opportunity to imagine otherwise.

The growth of the distance to Self and the own will makes the artificial person grow, which even one who has search for the own will's path can start holding for his own will, since the relation to the own will weakens and the feeling of selfhood in the artificial person's direction strengthens.

The growth of the distance to the own will is at the same time lowering of the consciousness, since only by lowering the consciousness is this possible.

Lost

When it is a question of a person, who already has started on the path of growing the own will, it is a question of unwillingness to confront a problem, or some problems, that he has encountered. Those problems have at some point, while growing the consciousness, risen up into the mind to some extent, and the person has chosen to avoid them.

Regarding other people it is also a question of unwillingness to confront, but their consciousness hasn't at any point been rising.

It is easier to start imagining to be free and independent in the wrong direction, than to really confront all obstacles and move in the right direction until one is truly freed.

Leaving the own will unfulfilled relieves the condition, since the obstacles that prevent the free motion doesn't appear. The person can experience the striving to fulfill free motion to be so heavy, that he neglects the fulfilling of the own will and concentrates in his strive to freedom only on inner experience.

Then the inner insight will in the end be flattened to thinking, and it will never rise up to where it was supposed to rise, and the freedom of the own will is left only as an experience in the imagination. A complete insight of something frees the person to fulfill that thing in the practical life.

In the present world people get a lot of support for this kind of escaping from oneself, and the feeling of freedom of motion, which grows by lowering the level of consciousness, feels easily as believable.

The clearest sign of this stray path is the joining to life on the level of consciousness of the world's thought, which is purely the artificial person.

The joining with it, in other words the growing of the bindings, connects the person with a growing strength to the world's thought, since his images of having reached something grows and his willingness to abandon that imaginary reached weakens.

If he abandons that image, he believes to lose something, even if he in fact doesn't lose anything, but is freed of something that prevents him from reaching what he originally wanted to reach.

Then the connection to the inner world and the approaching of Self weakens, and the connections to the ordinary world of the world's thought grows.

For a person that is truly on the path of the own will, all areas in life comply with the path of the own will, there are no exceptions.

The significance of the dominant thought

The dominant thought

The dominant thought means the thought that steers the activities of the individuals, a group or humanity as a whole. It is the thought that controls the persons in a certain area or a group in life.

Seen from Self's viewpoint, in other words from each and everyone's real will's viewpoint, the only right dominant thought is the individual's own free will.

The beings have together created a thought about life and its essence. Each and everyone has his own part in the whole, and the sum of all parts is the common thought for life to the extent of the whole humanity.

If we compare this thought created by the beings with what some might think of as god's will, we can only state that it is fully parallel even with that, due to the simple reason that the beings aren't in any way separate, but the unity of nearness created by a perfect mutual communication, all the way to the absolute truth.

To the extent of humanity, the purpose is fulfilled automatically, when the individuals are free in relation to their own wills and can fulfill them. They are aware of their own wills and seek to be entireties that fulfill the common will. This happens without hierarchical power, but it can't be fulfilled under hierarchical power.

The dominant thought in humanity is in this moment the hierarchical power structure, in which every decision about everything is such that it subjects the individuals' real wills. Society is a machinery, in which the parts have been forced to serve a machine that no one really wants. It is the forcing power of the centralistic thought, which doesn't approach any matter with respect to the individuals' own wills.

The thought of the free world

The thought of the free world has as premise that it supports every individual's own real will and gives it space. The beings are unanimous about creating life and everyone has a voluntarily chosen part in the entirety. The purpose of each and everyone is the self chosen task.

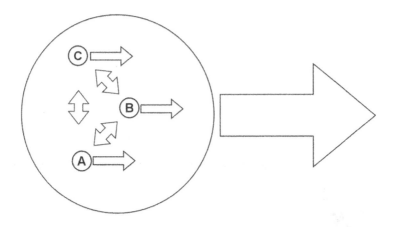

In the picture above is presented how the individuals A, B and C are communicating freely. Here they are unanimous about the direction of creating life and they all have their own part in fulfilling it. Their own wills are parallel with the total will, and they are free to fulfill their own wills as parts of the common will. It is the content of the original will of every human, and in the free world it is fulfilled.

In the centralistic thought a function model that reminds of this is understood as freedom. According to it, people can choose freely what they do. That freedom is in fact only apparent, since the needs are defined on the top of the hierarchy and with the help of the demand they produce, the possibilities in the choices are limited. In other words one can freely choose from the alternatives offered by the centralistic thought. One can't choose to completely abandon the influence of the centralistic thought.

The centralistic thought doesn't leave space to the influence of the own wills, which means that the feeling of freedom in it is an illusion, not real. That freedom is like a sandbox, where one has been told to sit and play. Most people also play in it nicely, since they experience other alternatives as such that they don't exist.

The centralistic world's thought

The centralistic thought functions with the system of hierarchical power, and in the systems that least suppresses the individuals, the goals of the activities are decided by a power that is chosen by the people.

The choice is only apparent, since people have been raised to a thought, where the hierarchical power is self-evident and is experienced to be the only alternative. The common choice concerns only who will decide about the contents of the centralistic thought. It doesn't concern the canceling of the centralistic power.

In the present world its sudden canceling would be quite impossible, since there aren't enough people in the world, whose own wills would function. The impossibility concerns both the canceling of the centralistic thought and the ability to fulfill the free world.

People consider problems of society to be matters that are a part of life. In fact, problems that aren't related to natural phenomena are problems caused by the centralistic thought. It is always imperfect and it can never be perfect, since it fundamentally is a lie.

The lie of the centralistic thought rests on the hierarchical power structure. It denies natural freedom and therefore it will never be the way to the perfect society.

Some try to create the perfect centralistic thought. That aim will always lead to strive for total control over people, which is the worst possible alternative.

People who believe the centralistic thought to be the only existing alternative, won't choose to cancel it. People that aren't their own persons with their own free wills, aren't capable of fulfilling a free world.

For that it wouldn't be enough even if half the society would have reached spiritual freedom. The other half wouldn't be able to function in a free society. Therefore the way to real freedom is long, and it can't be rushed to go faster than the rise of mankind's ability.

The jointly chosen centralistic government

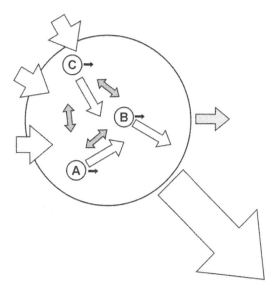

In the picture above, the thought of the community is controlled from the outside. It is influenced by the sum of several thoughts, since people have the possibility to, of the different alternatives, choose those who will decide the contents of the centralistic thought.

The individual A, B and C's' own thoughts can influence to some extent, since the power structure allows some degree of individual freedom. The activities of the individuals in the picture aren't completely decided by the centralistic thought, and therefore they have an apparent possibility to do things that serve other directions. The directions aren't however parallel with the own thought, and therefore their inner condition isn't balanced.

The small grey and two-headed arrows mean slight and bad communication. Bad in this context means that the communications aren't based on own wills, but generally happens in accordance with the seemingly free image of reality inside the boundaries of the centralistic thought.

Since the individuals' own wills have some space, even if not real possibility, the force of the individuals' own wills gets to influence the movement of the entirety to some extent. From that comes the small gray arrow, which shows the influence of the own wills in the community's path of motion.

The big white arrow, which starts in the circle, illustrates the force caused by the centralistic thought and which is absolutely the dominating factor on the community's path of motion.

The influence of the own wills is very small and the community's path of motion differs strongly from the direction of the sum of the own wills. People that haven't completely forgotten their own wills, experience this conflict as a bad feeling, even if they don't know the reason to it. For them it isn't possible to get satisfaction to life, since materialistic satisfaction or satisfaction given by imaginary values isn't enough for them.

Since the individuals' own wills have some space, and there exists apparent freedom, this society is quite stable. People accept it quite easily, since it doesn't cause very unbearable pain. If people's consciousness of themselves grows, they will influence the centralistic thought in such way that their freedom grows.

The more freedom the individual has, even if it is apparent freedom, the more stable this society is. Freedom makes the society strong even in the long term. This freedom is generally the freedom of the artificial person, and it brings satisfaction to the artificial person to the extent that the artificial person in question can experience freedom.

The idea of freedom is relative. If people's consciousness of self grows, they will experience the offered freedom as smaller and vice versa. In this community they can influence the centralistic thought and therefore it changes with the people.

Those who have lost the connection to themselves and have turned into artificial persons experience full satisfaction, since the thought model they have adopted is being fulfilled. In other words there is nothing in their minds that would be in conflict with the fulfilled. Those who still have an existing connection to self are the transformers of the fundamental thought of this community to the extent they are aware of themselves.

The centralistic autocracy

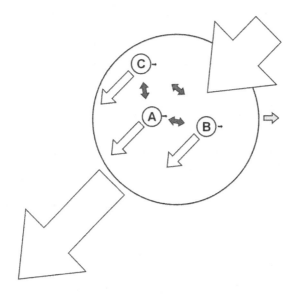

In this picture, the centralistic thought is autocracy, where all differing opinions and thoughts are forbidden. It decides very thoroughly the direction of every thought, and it forces all actions in the direction of the totalitarian centralistic thought. That is illustrated by the big white arrow on the top right side.

The existence on the individuals' own wills can't in any way be completely prevented, but with strong pressure they can be weakened to be nearly nonexistent. The very small black arrows, which start in the individuals, illustrate the very small influence of the own wills.

The communication between the individuals is very weak, since the centralistic thought prevents free communication in all its forms. This preventing of communication is meant to reduce the danger that people would rise up against the centralistic thought.

The own will's influence on the community's motion is still illustrated by the small gray arrow on the right side of the circle. It has an exceedingly small influence on the community's path of motion.

The white arrows, which start from the individuals, show how strongly the centralistic thought pressures everyone's actions in its forced direction. This way it is possible to build a community that has a lot of force in a certain direction.

There the direction of the individuals, as well as the community, is in a strong conflict with the direction of the individuals' own wills. In this community freedom is so limited that only a few persons, who have accepted the centralistic thought, can feel satisfaction of life inside it.

The more the community uses forcing as its method, the more unstable the community is in the long term and its lifespan is short. With time people will stop submitting to a thought that takes away even their slightest freedom of action.

These kinds of communities strive to be closed communities in order to prevent people from getting points of reference from the freedoms of other systems. The awareness of freer alternatives weakens the force of the centralistic power, and if it spreads, this awareness will overthrow the power of the centralistic thought.

Likewise free communication between people would bring up thoughts that differ from the thought offered by the centralistic power, and it would weaken the centralistic thought.

The instability of centralism

The centralistic thought goes from chaos to chaos and it never has balance, since it is based on power struggle, not on the natural free will.

It is the rulers struggle for their own power. That power struggle is conducted by many means. Some want absolute power for themselves, some are satisfied with a good position in the power hierarchy, and create apparent images to people of nice and good leaders, who think of everyone's best.

Common for all these are that they create lie, which fundamental purpose is to cover the real own will from people's consciousness and maintain their own position in the hierarchy. In fact, all people who accept the centralistic thought are the maintainers of it, those on the top as well as those on the bottom.

Depending of the extent of the feeling of freedom it creates, it is more stable or more unstable. The more people there are who experience the freedom it gives as believable and good, the more stable it is.

When some experience it to be pressuring in some way, they will start opposing it sooner or later. When enough people have the same opinion, they will influence it in a way that makes it change. The more the centralistic thought opposes the change, the greater possibility there is to a violent change. In that case it is also a question of a power struggle, since those who want changes, wants to change the centralistic thought, not to cancel it.

Those who maintain the centralistic thought have a very weak consciousness of themselves, in other words they can't see the actual lie, which is the crime against the natural freedom.

World's thought

The structure of the hierarchical power

There are many thoughts in the world, which define the human way of seeing himself, his environment, society and reality. These manifest themselves as cultures, which on the surface can feel very different. However, they have a mutual core, which is the "world's thought".

All the most significant cultures are built around the core of the world's thought. The cultures are just different ways of fulfilling the same thing. We might say that it is the same cake with different garnishing.

The present world's thought is the idea of hierarchical power, where society is controlled in a certain way from the top of the hierarchy. There exists different ways of how power is distributed, but the central idea is that power is distributed and its existence is held to be the only alternative. It is related to like to a law of nature that can't be questioned, and it is believed to be a part of the natural order.

The human is raised to bow for the power structure, and no alternatives are offered. Regardless if it is a question of upbringing at home, in schools or among religions, the influencer everywhere is the society's confessional core structure, which is the hierarchical power.

There isn't truly offered a free society that would offer a breeding ground for each person's original and from the self rising selfhood, and that would acknowledge the person's natural freedom to define his own life, his own choices, responsibilities and obligations.

Society

As a society is understood every unit of hierarchical power that is confessed as a state, or as any other administrative territory.

The society could as well be free and still be a society, but since such doesn't exist, we speak of the society as a society built under hierarchical power, if it isn't specifically mentioned that a free society is in question.

The premise is that the people inside the administrative territory are property of the administrative territory. People aren't said to be property of society but since society, in other words the power hierarchy, defines the freedom, rights and obligations of each human, it is a question of property.

The person himself doesn't have any say when defining them. Apparent right exists certainly, but even those rights have been defined by society, in other words the person isn't himself the one that ultimately defines his freedom, rights and obligations.

The society that exists in the present sense isn't something that occurs in nature, but is a by humans invented thought of an administrative unit that owns a large number of people.

Therefore society doesn't have any natural features, but is completely built out of the thoughts that are used to define what it is. So it is not based on the laws of nature and neither does it comply with them, but is in conflict with them.

It is a product of thinking, something that is invented by imagination and that can be altered and formed at will, unlimitedly. It doesn't in any sense have to be like, or function in a way, that it in some moment is or functions. For it is enough that it maintains the hierarchical power system.

The society's claimed right to control the individuals in some area isn't a right given by nature, but it is the subjecting mechanism of the persons who created the thought of society.

Someone might defend it by saying that it is defined by the majority, but in fact not a single individual's natural freedom can be taken by the decision of anyone. Making such decisions is forcing, not a right.

Secondly, the majority then referred to consists of people, who have been subjected to the hierarchical power.

As they are at present, the societies are built on the principle of forcing. They have at no point respected the natural freedom, and neither will they ever do that, since they originally have been built on the idea of forcing.

In the free society there also is a governing unit, but its nature isn't forcing, it only organizes common activities and has no power in the sense that the present society does, and which basic idea is power, or in other words forcing. The free society doesn't own anyone.

For those who are looking from the viewpoint of the system built on the idea of forcing power, it is quite impossible to see a system that is based on voluntary participation.

This simply since it is impossible for them to think that people voluntarily, and of their own wills, would form something that works.

This since one of their own basic thoughts about functionality is that it has to function as they want it to function. Moreover, their own position is built upon the existence of hierarchical power.

Regional freedom

States don't like the idea that their regions are free, since they see the use of power as the purpose of the state. States also implement the growth of their power by taking regions from each other in one way or another, if it by any means is possible. That creates a need for armed forces, regardless if it is a question of defending a region or attacking another region.

States are invented ideas, and they were originally born around armies as governmental systems, they don't exist in nature. In other words people maintain imaginary administrative areas, which build weapons to wage war with each other.

Since the original idea of states has been to subject others and to steal from them, the states experience as their own interest to take from everywhere anything that can be taken. They fulfill the principle of power struggle. There are different ways of implementing that principle, but basically the states still mostly act like robbers. It is more beautifully called for the states own interest.

Wars are therefore products of our own imagination, and we ourselves maintain them. We must notice, that everyone who accepts it and holds it to be true, is taking part in maintaining it. If no one maintains the thought, then it doesn't exist. It gets its strength from that people maintain it, regardless of the participating in the maintaining of it is submission or intense power struggle.

In the free world the governmental areas are simply meaningfully divided areas and the borders are moved, if the meaningfulness requires it. No permits are needed to cross the borders, since each and everyone can be where he wants. Their purpose is only to divide the land into meaningful areas of responsibility for the management of matters.

This description of the free world is only an approximate description of the free world's nature, not an instruction. When mankind is mature enough to step by step move to the free world, people will know what they are doing.

Regionally managed are such matters that are the common matters of the area. The freedom of the individuals isn't touched, since it is known to be an inexpedient action that isn't in anyone's interest, but against everyone's interest.

The society in the region is formed by voluntary participation to build the common area. It is the sum of the free wills of its inhabitants. It isn't controlled by the society, but the society's function is to contribute to improve the conditions and bring together different things, so that the wanted things can be fulfilled.

In this context those who lean on hierarchical forcing might in their mind get an image of confused activities, where everybody randomly does one thing or another.

In fact, truly free people are very rational and very capable to agree upon the cooperation in a way, where everything would function a thousand times better than anything has ever functioned in the history of mankind.

All people, whose own wills function, have their original wills that leads to good and is in advance compatible with other free wills.

The crucial difference in functionality is caused by the fact, that in the free society the original wills are freed to create the world we originally wanted to create.

In the society of hierarchical forcing even at its best, that is within the frames of the apparent democratic freedom, we can make solutions the majority can settle with, but that aren't completely good for anyone.

Some people experience that the community should have a strong leader for something to get done. People who long for that are regarding their own personal freedom in a condition, where they aren't capable of taking responsibility for it.

They are afraid to end up in a situation, where they would have to take responsibility for themselves and their real own wills. Therefore they gladly push away that responsibility from themselves and prefer to give themselves up as slaves for someone, who takes that responsibility from them.

Very often those who think like this are very intensively promoting the cause of the forcing power. The intensity is based on their fears.

They are afraid to take responsibility for themselves, and to get rid of that responsibility they want an outer strong power to subject them, so that they can feel safe. This way they can avoid the need to take responsibility for themselves.

At the same time others are bridled into the same order, and one doesn't have to fear that they break that order. The breaking of that order feels for one who supports forcing power as a threat to his own capability to get along with others.

People like this are excellent supporters to the power-hungry, who have caused the greatest disasters of mankind.

The lust for power, and the forcing of others, of the power-hungry is based on the same phenomenon as for the mentioned supporters of forcing power. The only difference is their position in the power hierarchy.

There can always be found those who enjoy power, and who try to convince that they are taking responsibility for matters and there can always be found those, who will gladly give away the responsibility for themselves to others.

In fact, within the power hierarchy no one takes responsibility for anyone's real will. Not even those who are in power are taking responsibility for anything real. Responsibility is defined as responsibility for the hierarchical power system, and for the goals and values defined by it.

The time of the free society is here when people themselves take responsibility for themselves, and ceases to have a dependency relation to the thoughts about rulers and the hierarchical power system.

Taking responsibility starts with that the person focuses on his inner freedom, and on finding his own will. He has to grow to be capable in fulfilling his own will and the purpose of his life.

Welcome to this world

In the present environment it is very difficult for a child who still remembers his original self and will, in other words the purpose of his life, to preserve even a weak connection to his own real self.

The environment strives to program the child to fit into their imagined society, and in no case do they help the child's inner own self to develop into being the fulfiller of his own will. The child is seen as a piece of support for the existing system and its purposes, not at all as an independent being who has an existing own purpose regarding his own life.

The cultures

Quite few create thoughts, or partial thoughts, that form the offered cultures. The majority of people learn some thought and acts in accordance with it, and fit their life's choices into the frames of that thought or culture.

The culture is formed out of ways of life, valuations and goals. It is the agreed framework for living, and the way to fulfill it. It appears in art, science and everything that concerns life.

For us to be able to upon Alkuajatus build a thought that people follow, we have to create a culture that is made for it. That culture will rise from the freed doers of art and science, who find new viewpoints.

Without any culture people wouldn't have any life model to fulfill. No matter how allowing, supportive to versatility and in favor of the individuals complete freedom the culture is, it still needs to exist.

A culture is an agreement on the courses of action and it reflects the basic ideas of thinking. A culture that makes complete freedom possible is also a culture, even if its rules differ from the presently existing cultures so that it offers real freedom to act in accordance with the own will.

When the culture somewhere in the future forms to be the culture of the free world, then it is the world's thought of that time. Then the dominant thought in the world is Alkuajatus, which really doesn't define anything else, but that the own will's thought is the right thought of each time.

Then the world's thought will form in full balance in accordance with the level of truth that is dominant in that time. Its change is natural and continuous, not the result of battles.

That world is very stable, since own wills don't randomly run after this and that, but are clear and purposeful.

The world's thoughts are games that are played. They aren't true, but they are agreements of the ways to think and act. The presently dominant thoughts are all built for the needs of maintaining hierarchical power.

There are winners and losers among people, and they are all a part of that thought with their own roles. The human participates in it by accepting it as the fundamental thought for his life, no matter what position he has in the hierarchy. It is maintained together, whether we like it or not.

The maintained system is built for the needs of using power. The power that is being fought over is a pursuit for selfish needs, regardless if it is a question of a group or an individual. Whoever has the possibility to in the name of the achieved power exercise the so called pursue of own interests, he will do so.

As the cohesive force in hierarchy is the thought that society must be controlled in accordance with some will that is in power. It gives society the right to force individuals under its power and define the responsibilities of the individuals.

It is assumed that society, to be able to cohere, needs the cooperation of all individuals in a way that is defined by power. This assumption bypasses the possibility that society would function as the sum of the wills of free individuals.

The wills of free individuals are even considered to be dangerous, since they are experienced to be destructive to society. It is true in the sense that they are destructive to that society, since the society in question doesn't control the thoughts and wills of the free individuals.

Many experience this as frightening and therefore they want to support the centralistic world's thought, in other words the hierarchical power. The fear is based partly on the fear of the own inner world, and partly on a misunderstanding regarding what the own will really means.

Let us do an example about the nature of the free will:

The person has a house, where he lives with his family. In the present world the house is locked, since otherwise a thief would take everything without permission. It is thought that the thief is fulfilling his own will. In fact, the thief is confused and fulfills the system of power hierarchy, as do the states.

In the world of free will people aren't confused, but the will is the inner and original own will in a free form. It respects the wills of others and helps them. It never harms them. Then there is no need for locks on the houses and the only purpose of doors is to keep the cold, animals and insects on the outside.

The centralistic thought, in other words the present world's system that is experienced as the normal society, is continuous power struggle where there is no natural freedom and never will be. The power game isn't a product of mankind's free wills. It is a way of thinking we have learned over thousands of years.

It was started by persons who began to subject others to their power. It started as forcing and it has been refined into a way of thinking that is learned at a very young age, in other words the human is brought up into a culture that recognizes the right of centralistic power.

The upbringing into the arms of the centralistic will teaches the child to satisfy the needs of the thought that is in control, and to reject his own original will. It teaches him to choose the right things from the selection that the system maintains. It is impossible to make choices in accordance with the own will since those aren't offered, and the individual has at no stage been given an opportunity to grow into them himself.

This trap in the upbringing has functioned and been developed for so long, that it has been accepted as a self-evident part of life to the extent, that already the questioning of it is considered to be strange and a very unreal alternative. People who are in the viewpoint of this upbrought thought can't think in any other way, but by holding it to be the only possible way of seeing society.

They are afraid of other alternatives. Other alternatives might for instance be seen as anarchistic disorders that only cause arbitrary and destruction. It is impossible for them to think that the model of society, which at the present is centralistic, isn't the guarantee for balanced and stable development, but the maintainer of imbalance and instability.

If we look at the history of the world, we can clearly see how much violence and imbalance there has existed around the world. The stronger the hierarchical command structure, the more violent and arbitrary the life of the society is, even towards its own individuals.

In many democracies, where the free area of the individuals has been slightly increased, there is more stability, but inside them there is still imbalance and less happy life.

The only balanced and stable system is the agreed cooperation that rises from the individuals own free choices, and that binds the individuals in a way they have chosen and in matters they have chosen.

This sounds frightening to one who has been brought up to hierarchical power, since no one decides for everyone, but everyone takes responsibility for himself, his will and his actions. The final result is the sum of free wills and not some will outside the individuals, which according to the ideas of the present system is the right and reasonable way to control the development.

Free development is development and cooperation that happens on an individual level. Its result can't be decided by any centralistic power. Its results are what they are, and they are good.

Centralism is considered necessary for the activities to be controlled. When it is a question of the individuals' free wills, they are already compatible, if they only are free.

Free wills create entireties, and factors that bind to the activities, with their own strength and in their own way. They don't need an outer power, which only messes the freedom of the wills.

Wills that are created before birth are in complete harmony with each other, and a doer will be found for every part, if everyone gets to grow up to be his own self. They are already at birth persons who have come to build entireties, and they carry the plan inside them.

An earthly centralistic system is only necessary for the purpose of subjecting individuals. Those in power, and those who enjoy power, will lose their positions and power the day when the world is free and the original self controls each and everyone's life.

Narrowing of freedom, moving the power of decision

Even if exercising power in the ancient times was in average a lot more violent than today, the rulers grip of the citizens was considerably much weaker than today. Even then the power tried to get the best possible grip, but the tools were more inadequate.

Especially in the developed democracies those in power have strongly tightened their grip on people. The own freedom of people has been reduced and it has been changed into decision making power for those in power. The person's own decision making power considering his life has weakened and the power's grip of people has grown stronger.

An increasing proportion of the person's production and time is, instead of himself, decided by society and the ways of thinking that it breeds. His responsibilities and obligations are decided by laws. His own will has been displaced in many ways, very thoroughly, and he has become property of society instead of an independent and free person.

The control is very much justified with the safety of people. Those who justify it with safety are actually the original reason to that insecurity. They maintain and try to strengthen the idea of hierarchical power, which is the reason to the power struggle, criminality and wars, which all are expressions of it.

It is also justified with the welfare of society, and as excuses are used for instance education, healthcare, aid to the poor and many other things that are seen as good. Goodness has very little to do with these things. Society wants to control them, partly to be able to monitor them and partly to grow people's dependence on society.

The hierarchical power system doesn't do acts of compassion, it does whatever it does for itself, to strengthen its power. The idea of power is to strive to the growth and the strengthening of power.

The individual is tied to society in many ways, so that he can't manage without the tutelage of society. The deeper society's power over the individual goes, the better this dependency can be used as a justification to that society has a great power over the individual.
The more the power of decision shifts to society, the more dependent people are of it, and therefore also those in power. This way it can produce an easily controlled human herd, which is its goal.

In the present world there are several countries that are controlled by democracy. They are seemingly free, since the subjecting of people isn't as visible forcing as in less democratic countries.

In fact, the power's grip on people is at least as tight, but it has only been implemented by teaching the people to be the system's sheep. There is no longer a need for the sword as the tool of power against the citizens of the country.

The most significant enemy to hierarchical power is the free individual, since one who is truly free, in other words one that has found his will and himself, can't be controlled.

Therefore the power is of the view, that this connection to Self must disappear. This disappearance of the connection is executed with lies that cover the truth.

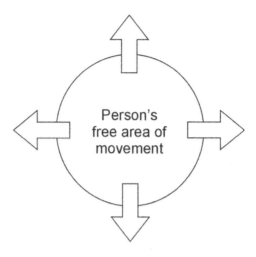

In this picture the person has freedom of movement to expand his world and to act in accordance with his original will, without any outer misleading, forcing or any other strive to restrict.

The premise should be that the person's own will controls his own life. Then his will is free to move and the only obstacles are for instance in the understanding of how the material world functions, and the obstacles of the growth of the own consciousness. The obstacles aren't based on that someone is lying and tries to confuse, but they are so to speak normal problems.

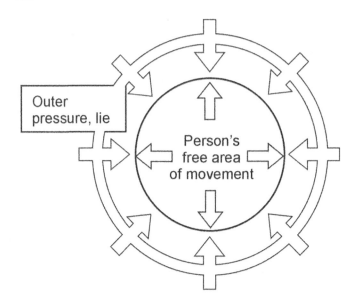

The picture above illustrates how the pressure from the environment strives to limit the person's free area of movement. The only way to limit it is to lie. Even if it is not understood to be lying, that is it still.

Freedom is limited by all lies, with which help the person's right to natural freedom is weakened. Their purpose is to exclude the person's own original will. Those without their own will are easy to control and to program into suitable concepts of reality and values, which all serve the hierarchical power system.

The outer pressure and the lie are partly the ways of thinking, which already a long time ago have been forced into people's minds, and which move from one generation to the next through the upbringing. Partly they are the present everyday life, where the increasing of the power's grip is justified with things that can feel believable, but which are not true.

This is impossible to understand for a person, who has fully lost his connection to himself, since he isn't capable of recognizing the existence of the original own will. For him the own will is a collection of thoughts that has been built out of the thought models he was taught, maybe spiced with some own development work.

Those who still have a connection to the own will at some level can recognize this phenomenon, and understand it to be true. From that there is still some way to finding the own will and to understand Self, whose approaching is a prerequisite to see this.

Among the young there are a lot of those, who still experience the connection. It disappears when the person decides to bow into being an adult in accordance with the world's thought. For some it is preserved for a very long time, even throughout life.

The narrowing of freedom is something that is done gradually, so that the persons would submit to it in a way where they accept it themselves. One who tries to limit freedom asks for a little at a time, and trusts that the person will rather bargain a little of his freedom, than to have to see the trouble of opposing.

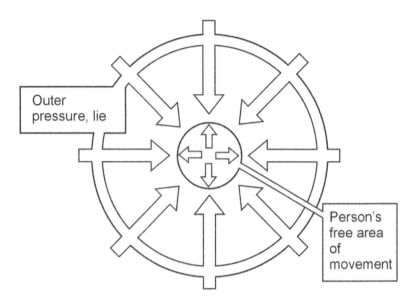

This way freedom is gradually narrowed and people are more than before under the power of those, who practice that power.

The narrowing of freedom is experienced as good only by one who wants to control others, or who wants that someone else takes his own responsibility from him. The consequence of this is that the decision making power of the individual's life is moved away from himself.

People in many countries get more free time and even entertainment. These create an illusion of freer living. A person, who isn't a problem for the power, can in his free time do what pleases him, since his own will has been exterminated a long time ago.

He believes to do what he wants, but he is acting inside the boundaries set by the power. He consumes entertainment for his pleasure to forget that life in fact doesn't give him the satisfaction, which solely and exclusively the own free will can give.

This way people are moving towards the "ideal society", where they all are children in society's bosom, and who are always having fun, and never has any responsibility. Spiritually it is slavery, a pleasant trap which one falls into, since taking responsibility feels so heavy.

The difference between hierarchical world power and the free world

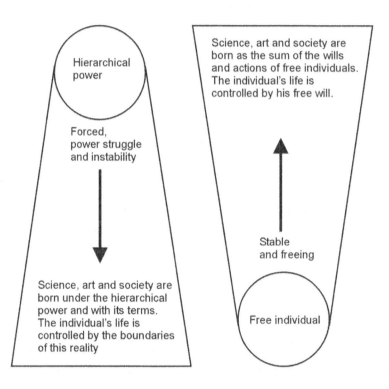

The picture illustrates the difference between the free world and the hierarchical world.

The hierarchical power system suppresses the free will, since it strives to define the needs and purposes in centralistic manner.

The bigger freedom the people in this system have, the more creative and viable it is. Changes in this system are results of power struggles.

The free world doesn't in centralistic manner decide the needs and purposes. It is the sum of the free wills of free individuals.

The individuals' wills, when complying with the real own will, are compatible and those who support the same things seek to cooperate by themselves.

Their thoughts are compatible to form entireties and the society is completely stable, since there is no conflict between the intensions.

The development and changes of society happen in accordance with the development of the individuals' wills.

Development is always something that causes some degree of pain. The free world and its harmony doesn't necessarily mean a painless society. The higher and clearer the consciousness rises in average, the more painless and harmonic the entirety will be.

Let us repeat here, that the free world requires a sufficient level of consciousness from mankind. Its acquisition could in principle happen quite fast, since the ability of people would be sufficient for it. But as a resistance there are many subjecting forces and the ignorance of people. Therefore a very fast change shouldn't be expected. In theory a few decades could be enough, but in reality it can be a question of a hundred or hundreds of years.

Everyone who grows his consciousness has a positive influence on his environment and the coming generations in a way, where they reduce the burden of the lies as a whole, and that way makes it easier for others to start growing their consciousness.

The change towards the free world is gradual. It can't be founded with laws, and it can't be achieved with a revolution.

The only path is the freeing of the individuals and the growth of consciousness. Each and everyone must take responsibility for himself, no one can force anyone to free himself and no one can free himself for anyone.

When this kind of development has changed the world into a free world, the world's thought is also free.

Relativity of the world's thought

The world's thought is relative.

The world's thought in each time is a different thought, than the thought of the own wills of the children who are born.

The world's thought can change in a more untruthful or a more truthful direction, and in both cases its level of truth is weaker than the thought of the born new wills.

Even when the world's thought one day is very close to the ground rules of inner reality, its level of truth is still weaker than the thought of the new wills that have come to raise the level of consciousness.

The world's thought exists as long as there exist finiteness, since as long as there exist finiteness, the consciousness can be grown compared to before.

In the present world the level of lie is great and because of that the level of consciousness is weak. A born human doesn't get help in the direction of his own will in order to grow to be his own person and to fulfill his own original will. He is mislead by the world's thought and grows up to be a person, who is far away from his own original thought.

While the world's level of consciousness rises, the world gradually changes into a place, where the born new thoughts get sufficient help in order to develop in their intended way. Then the lie of the world's thought in relation to the born own wills isn't great, and it is fully possible for the persons to develop directly, without bends, in the direction of their own wills.

In Alkuajatus we speak of the world's thought that is prevailing in the present time, unless it is specifically stated otherwise.

Religions

Where religions came from

Originally religion was the person's inner experience and what controlled his life, each and everyone had a working own inner religion-function. At that time the world was still free and the beings created lives controlled by their own wills.

Later on came persons, who began to violently subject other persons into the circle of their stealing. This stealing was later called taxation right and these thieves came to be called kings. Gradually people were taught to submit and accept as a fact the formed hierarchical power system.

To the born apparatus of power it was a problem that religion was an inner matter to people and that it controlled life. The independence of people wasn't experienced to be a good thing, since controlling independent people is laborious and sometimes even impossible.

Therefore those in power favored religions, with which religion was outsourced. Thus was born the religions and churches controlled by priests, who instead of the religion-function offered the stories they teach and outer power.

One could think that people abandoned their religion-function. It is also so, but the most significant reason is that those, who were supposed to take care of the development of the religion-function and the existence of the knowledge, yielded to the hierarchical power system. If the religion-function would have been taken better care of, this birth of outer power would never have happened.

The origin of the stories in the religions varies depending on the religion. Naturally they tell and assure to be authorized by their god. God and gods were concepts that were needed as outer authorities to replace the natural inner connection to the truth.

The thought-images offered by the religions tell of hierarchical heavens, since the rulers had to be able to justify themselves as the continuation of heavenly power.

One can wonder how many kings, priests and other representatives of authority have been assigned by God or gods, and as it happens, the people has to be obedient to the authorities.

As a result of this the subjected people forgot themselves and their own personal religion-functions. Instead of it they built into their minds a collection of thought-images, which were based on the imaginary stories taught by the religions.

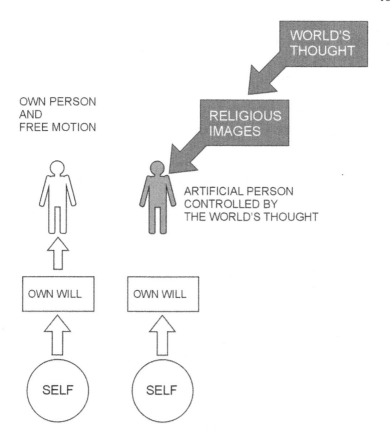

The modern man grows up to believe in the stories that are told. He believes in them, since he has been taught to believe in them. When he looks for inner answers, he looks in the wrong place. He looks for answers in the collection of thought-images in his mind instead of using his natural channel to the truth, in other words the religion-function.

These collections are as thought-images quite effective. They can be used to generate emotional states that feel genuine, even if they only are based on comparisons between learned thoughts and ideas created by the products of the imagination.

Religious images can be replaced by atheistic images that strengthen the belief in the materiality of reality. The purpose of the religions is fulfilled also with those, which is the suppression of people's religion-function.

Are religions the cause of miracles?

Religions are supported to some degree by that when a human very strongly believes in something, he might succeed with performances that are considered to be miracles or unbelievable achievements. This firm belief is strong, and it doesn't as a function fall because it is explained incorrectly. This way the religions can get unmerited honor and people's belief in the thought-images grows stronger.

If we for instance compare healings caused by belief, we can discover that it is quite indifferent what the person believed in. There is no difference what he believed in. It is a question of an ability that is part of the natural proclivities of the human, nothing stranger than that.

So religions have nothing to do with those phenomena, and not one religion can arrogate those to themselves as products of their religion.

Or can anyone seriously claim that a person who has eaten a sugar pill, and who believes to have been given medicine and heals, has a religious explanation for what happened the same way as one who believed in some saint explains to have been healed by the force of prayer.

By comparing these it is very evident that the healing is caused by the belief in something, but without any connection to any religion.

Corrections

The stories about hierarchical heavens are connected to the power hierarchy's ways of thinking. They strive to form images so that the hierarchical power system would be believed to be a truthful system. The only purpose of these images is to suppress the original own will and freedom.

There exists no sin. No action itself is bad or good. Each action is only an action. From the action comes a consequence and only the consequence is important. If the consequence is good, the action was right, regardless of what the action was.

When evaluating the consequences of the action, we must consider all its consequences, which include all viewpoints that are connected to it. If the consequences of the action contain a lot of bad and a little good, it was a foolish action. The more good there is in the consequences, the more reasonable it was.

There is no original sin or any other burdens that one should carry with him. Each and everyone is the prisoner of his own confusion and unconsciousness. No other burdens exist.

There doesn't exist any saints or any other beings that should be worshiped. Only those who are unaware of the truth can imagine such. These kinds of fantasies can be found in the religions that are formed to be tools of power.

Repentance is useless. If some action brings a bad result, the only useful way to relate to it, is to learn from it and correct what can be corrected. When one learns to do the same action without any error, the actual problem is corrected and the pain related to it disappears.

There doesn't exist judgments, heavens or hells. The judgment is done by each and everyone himself. With foolishness one provides his own hell and by growing the consciousness his heaven, if we want to use those words to describe the matter.

The road to "hell" goes through the lowering of the own consciousness, which is equal to irresponsibility. From irresponsibility follows the lowering of consciousness and through the growth of confusion non-functionality of life.

The road to "heaven" goes through growing the own consciousness, which is equal to responsibility. From that follows through the rise of consciousness and clarification a more functional life.

Many religions offer salvation as a product of belief, but there is no other salvation than to restore the own religion-function and to reach the true self and the own will. It is the restoring and growth of consciousness.

There doesn't exist a law of karma that binds the beings, neither as the plus of former good actions or as the minus of the bad ones.

No good action makes the person wiser. Not a single error in the own person is corrected by good actions. The growing of the person's level of truth, in other words the growth of wisdom, is the only way to become free. The problem that earlier led to a mistake is then corrected, and that is the only thing of relevance.

The reflection of actions upon oneself sooner or later, in accordance with the law of karma, is in a way correct. The reason is that to be able to correct the problem, Self brings the problem that caused the action before its person in its try to solve it.

The reason to that the action is reflected upon the own person later in one way or another, isn't in the action itself, but the problem that causes the action.

Self can restrict the person so that the consequence of the problem, in other words the action, doesn't repeat itself, but nor does that solve the problem. It only hides the problem and at the same time it reduces the own person's freedom of movement, in other words the consciousness.

Even if one has done the same foolish action a thousand times, and the same action would be directed on the person in one way or another, the problem needs to be solved only once. Then the matter has been dealt with and responsibility has been taken.

The problem that caused the foolishness can never be avoided, since the route to freedom and the growth of consciousness requires the correction of all errors in the own person.

Carrying out foolishness consciously is a fast way to lower your consciousness and create problems for your future, and a lot of problems that are difficult to confront and which you can't escape.

Foolishness that isn't conscious is out of reach for the consciousness only because the being has earlier lowered its consciousness regarding the foolishness in question.

No compensative actions are needed, since when the person is his own will's person, he will in any case produce as much good as possible by his nature.

The only important thing is that the person returns to his own real will, and fulfills it in accordance with the best of his ability.

The religion-function

The religion-function

The human doesn't need a religion such as religions are thought of in the present world. The human needs the religion-function, which is his natural inner function.

Religions as they are thought of presently are something outside of the human, and something that is unfortunately much used to control people.

The religion-function is the channel between the person's conscious level and the real selfhood, and what functions as his connection to his origin, in other words Self.

The person doesn't need an outer organization, anyone's blessing or authority, or even anyone's permission or acceptance. The only thing he needs is the connection to Self, the own will, the original selfhood.

In liberation it is a question of reopening the lost connection, nothing else.

This connection is the religion-function, it is not a religion. It has no shape, custom or a certain form. Its essence is consciousness, which in no way is dependent of anything. It is consciousness of the real selfhood, that is all it is.

Alkuajatus is a religion, since it materially exists and is a thought of spiritual liberation, and a thought that concerns inner reality.

But Alkuajatus is not a religion that positions itself as an outer controlling factor. It is a guide that helps to find the religion-function, to free the own original will.

The religion-function could be called a personal religion, but this definition wouldn't correspond very well with its true nature, since a religion would be a defined thought, and the religion-function is unlimited.

The religion-function can't be formed into words, since it is not finite and words are finite. Neither can it be presented as a picture, sound or in any other limited form. It is not limited, since it is the original consciousness that is the voice of Self inside each and everyone.

Selfhood can express itself in many ways, but still be the same thing.

Every created thing, all that is limited, is the expression of selfhood to the extent that selfhood influences it.

The world is selfhood's modeling clay and life is selfhood's fulfilling.

The purpose of selfhood is to express itself as well as possible and without obstacles.

To the extent that selfhood is expressed freely, its product is good.

Behind almost every thought that later on formed into a religion, the original idea was to make the human approach Self, no matter with what name it is called. What was originally meant with god, in those that have the concept god, is in fact equal to Self.

Later on those thoughts served as a foundation to religions, whose original idea was to bring people under the power of the created religion.

The power in those is spiritual power with which people's thinking, and therefore also their lives, is controlled.

We can't deny the existence of divinity, since divinity is a synonym to the state of consciousness of the absolute truth. As concepts God and divinity are so far away from the human ability to reach and understand, that the pondering over the whole question can't bring anything else but wrong answers, so it is more wise not to ponder.

Seen from the human viewpoint, only the reaching of Self is meaningful. Before finding himself, the human has no possibility to understand the least of what divinity is and means.

The great teachers were interested in opening the inner function, not power, but the truth. They were teachers, guides. They used their religion-function to raise their consciousness.

The truth is never on the outside, the truth is not in written texts, and the truth is not in the spoken words.

The truth is always an inner matter, it is inner insight, without which the person has no connection to it.

At best the written text or the spoken word is a good description of the landscape that each and everyone must find by observing the inside.

The person has understood and knows the truth only to the extent he finds it inside him. What he doesn't find there, is either lie or for the moment unreached truth.

The person's religion-function works on the level provided by his consciousness and clearness.

Learn to listen to yourself

The religion-function could be described as listening to oneself. Then one quiets down, is relaxed and without thought. This doesn't mean voices on the inside, but the feeling that is the silent voice on infinity, which is the voice of Self.

To be able to hear himself, the person must be honest to himself. It isn't possible to get deeper in the truth than one is honest to oneself, and therefore capable of understanding the truth. No one can see something he closes his eyes to.

It is necessary to get an insight about what honesty to oneself means. It can't be understood by observing the matter from the viewpoint of the sense of selfhood formed out of thoughts, since that is one of the lies that has to be revealed and made to disappear.

Listening to Self is experiencing and feeling selfhood, not thinking.

While listening to Self one must be fully open to see the lies and false ideas in one's mind. One must not hold on to anything. Nothing must be hidden or defended. One has to dare to experience Self, who is in the truth.

When the touch of this is sufficient, the person grows stronger in listening to himself and in creating his own life with a greater freedom.

This ability to listen to oneself grows gradually into being present in every moment of the everyday life.

Avoid self-deception

In self-deception the person ceases to listen to himself. He closes his eyes to the lies and refuses to see them.

In that case he is protecting things in life that are based on lies, since he from the untruthful viewpoint experiences the preservation of those lies to be necessary.

Seen from that viewpoint, the revealing of the lies would lead to painful losses and changes, which he would experience as too difficult.

In self-deception the person imagines to be honest to himself, since he determinately refuses to see the lies that he from his viewpoint experiences to be difficult.

In that condition he limits his consciousness to be able to experience that he is honest to himself, and this limiting of the consciousness is the prerequisite for the protecting of the lies.

This way he prevents himself from growing his consciousness, and he remains tied to the level of consciousness that doesn't yet reveal those lies.

Then he has abandoned the route to freedom, and has started to build imaginary images to be able to preserve his idea of that he is an honest seeker on his way towards the truth.

One who truly seeks the truth is ready to confront anything and to lose everything, since he is fully aware of that only the truth will set one free, and that in the abandoning one can never lose anything else but lies.

The danger of self-deception is always present, since the world's thought supports it and easily makes it look tempting. The lies one gets caught in can according to the world's thought, in other words according to the artificial person, be very important and valued.

If the reason for self-deception is in human relations, it might be based on that the person doesn't want to abandon the feeling he has toward someone on that level of consciousness. The raising of consciousness could reveal the lies that feeling is based on, and therefore the preservation of the lies is the prerequisite for the preserving of that feeling.

Concerning human relations there also is a danger to get caught in wishing. Then the person wishes to be able to reach a certain relation, or to maintain a certain relation, by limiting himself.

Self-deception is fulfilled also by that the person experiences a specific person to be so important, that it for that person's sake is justified to diminish oneself.

In fact, in that case the person abandons his own real will and chooses the viewpoint of the artificial person. He is then lying to himself, as well as others.

If it in question is a relation that is based on the truth, it doesn't have to be protected from the truth.

Not a single thing that can't withstand the truth is based on the truth.

The characteristics of self-deception are choices that aren't based on the own will. Choices that serve the growth of the lie, bind to the world's thought or slow down the own freeing, are never based on the own real will.

The characteristics of the own will are actions that increase both one's own and others inner freedom as well as possible, and with the best possible speed.

Guide

Inner guide

The inner guide is infallible.

The inner guide takes care of the person's correct direction and the necessary development in life. It is a function that steers life from a deeper level than the experienced conscious level. Each and everyone has his own, and in each case it takes care of the own relation to the own purpose and the own life.

The inner guide is ultimately equal to Self, since Self is the one who is conscious. Self is aware of the condition of the own person compared to its will. When Self tries to decrease this distance, the own person senses the steering, which from his viewpoint seen is coming from the highest possible level of consciousness. The person is capable of sensing the steering as a feeling, but he is not on the level of consciousness the feeling originates from.

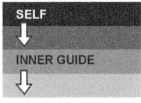

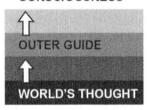

In this picture Self is, from the person's viewpoint seen, in unconsciousness, since he isn't capable of experiencing anything from Self's pure viewpoint. Self influences however so that the person hears his own voice from the highest possible viewpoint. This hearing is a feeling the person senses.

At the same time the surrounding world offers different life advice and temptations to the person. These advice and temptations, whose influence distances the person from himself, are so to speak the trap of the world's thought. Its objective is to get the person into the viewpoint of the world's thought.

In the present world most people fall far away from themselves and lose the contact to themselves in their younger years. Then the inner guide stops functioning and as the inner guide steps aside, it is gradually replaced by an outer guide.

By the outer guide we mean those thoughts that distance from Self and pull the person into the boundaries of the world's thought.

When the person can't see clearly, he deviates from the direction defined by his own will, or he falls behind on the timetable that is in accordance with his purpose. Then he, inside him, feels the growth of the distance compared to his own will. From that follows unease, which magnitude is equal to the deviation. In the case of a small error the unease can be of the size of a weak sense.

The person doesn't necessarily see what it is, but he feels that something isn't right. The purpose is that he addresses the matter, and clarifies to himself what didn't go right and corrects the error. This way he will always find the right route and the correct speed for his movement in life.

The reason to that he doesn't see something clearly is the lack of knowledge regarding some matter, or some lie that he hasn't revealed to himself.

The correcting of the lack of knowledge is done by looking into the matter so well, that the lack of knowledge is corrected. The revealing of the lie is done by focusing on the matter for so long, that one can see what in it isn't true. In both cases one might need both the acquisition of knowledge and observation of the matter.

If the problem doesn't get solved, the one and only reason is that the person doesn't focus on it enough, in other words he doesn't take the sufficient responsibility for the matter.

Responsibility in the matter is that the person doesn't hold on to any lies by oversight, or because he would like to hold for truth something he doesn't want to abandon. When it is a question of some knowledge or skill, the usual threshold question is the unwillingness to sufficiently focus on the matter. The person would like to achieve a result with less effort than what is required to achieve the result.

The nuisance of falling into self-deception is constantly present. It is fed by the desire to strengthen the existing ideas instead of complete openness. The falling is also favored by the fear of that the new discovery can demolish the structure of the earlier world of perceptions. A too hasty desire to decide for oneself that this is enough is the most excellent hiding place, in other words a notch to fall into.

The inner guide is very infallible, it is perfect. The feeling it produces, which can solve every problem if it is followed, is pure to the extent the person's mind is near his own will's person.

The pureness can only be maintained by a constantly growing honesty towards oneself. The seed of the lie in life is the inner dishonesty toward oneself.

From inner guide to the accuser and outer guide

Self has a natural desire and ability to be correct in its actions and knowledge. It doesn't want to be right just for the sake of it, but it wants to be right in its choices to fulfill its own will.

When the own person doesn't function correctly compared to it, the reason is that the person doesn't see clearly. It makes the person deviate from the own will's direction that was created by Self. Then the person experiences the unease caused by the growth of distance, he knows deep within himself that something didn't go right.

He can't see what it is, but that unease is supposed to make him look for the reason to it and to correct it. When he consequently seeks and finds an error and corrects it, he remains in the direction set by the own will.

As a child he confidently copies the knowledge of his environment. He expects to be given help for the development of his own will, but he is waiting in vain. He can't define what is happening, but he experiences the growth of the distance.

Since the offered knowledge are lies from the world's thought, and not knowledge that acknowledges the own will and Self, he can't approach his true own will.

Instead he builds his own person, in accordance with the false knowledge, towards a person built on the base of the world's thought, in other words the artificial person. Confidently he believes to do the right thing, but still he is left with a bad feeling.

The offered knowledge is such that it excludes the own will and even Self. It is knowledge that steers towards the ideas of the world's thought, in other words the person distances from his own will when he uses that knowledge. The given knowledge doesn't usually deny the existence of the original own will and Self, it only remains silent about them until they are dead. No support for the own will can be found and it makes him feel despair.

The natural desire to make correct choices, and to develop in fulfilling the own will, is searching for inner satisfaction that confirms the right direction. When the world's thought is in control, this natural search for satisfaction is easily transformed into the pleasing of other people, with which one looks for outer acceptance and support for that the chosen direction and actions are correct.

The world's thought favors the growth into being an artificial person, and the replacing of the own original will with the will that the artificial person experiences. It has in the reality controlled by the world's thought been defined as free will. The freedom there is inside the boundaries of the reality provided by the world's thought, and in accordance with its values.

If the person doesn't give up the connection to himself and his own will, he experiences a desire to be on his way towards the direction of his own will, but he ends up in the direction of world's thought. This is caused by that the only directions he can fulfill, are the directions learnt from the world's thought. He wants to go in some direction, but is driven in another direction. This makes the confusion grow and it leads to insecurity and self-accusations.

The base for self-accusations is born out of that no matter how right he would do in accordance with the give instructions, he ends up in the wrong direction compared with what he really wants. He doesn't want to go in the offered direction, since it doesn't feel right, but he can't build his life with anything else but the given advice, and he has to do something.

The child can't reveal the world's lie even if he would experience it to be wrong, when he notices that it doesn't lead in the right direction. He wants to go in a different direction than where the world's thought strives to take him, but he is powerless.

While the own will's attraction still is great, he fails with every effort to adapt to the thought provided by the environment, since he doesn't learn to lie to himself.

Eventually he loses the fight for his own will, but neither does he submit to the world's thought. He is left in the middle ground, and he can't fully live in either world. He can't reach what he wants and he doesn't experience the offered world as his home. This kind of person has preserved a quite good connection to himself.

Most people jump out of this development by striving to forget themselves. Mostly it succeeds gradually while growing towards adulthood. Some give up earlier, some later. In any case they become, in accordance with the ideas of world's thought, decent and responsible adults.

For some the forgetting is strong, but it is never complete.

Those who don't fully succeed in forgetting themselves are

plagued by uncertainty, and the connection to self still exists. They can be left in a condition where they desperately try to get approval to support their connection to the world's thought, which they can't fully reach.

Persons who won't forget themselves but hang on to it discover that they are incapable of the life and the values that are experienced as normal. There exists no compatibility.

They can't freely be what they want to be, since they can't well enough remember what it is. They can't become a part of the ordinary life, since it doesn't interest them, and they are incapable of lying to themselves enough to be able to take part in the theater. They feel like they are stuck between wood and bark. They can't reach the own and the so called normal life doesn't give the desired challenge or satisfaction.

From an early age the person has experienced how the direction and the will, which he feel inside him, aren't at all consistent with the offered world. Since he doesn't have the strength to be right, the world's thought is given a strong role in being right, and gradually the truth offered by the world's thought grows, even inside him, to be stronger than the truth of the own will. This changed base of comparison considers the will he remembers as foolish and his maladjustment to the world's thought as a lack of ability.

This way the inner guide becomes the inner accuser and the person might be in a constant state of self-accusations. The accuser tells him how bad and incapable he is, and how useless and negligible he is. This turns his life into suffering, and might ruin his whole life.

The accuser is a collection of untruthful knowledge that has clouded Self's evaluation of the person's life and created an untruthful evaluation. Therefore the feeling the person experiences is born out of an incorrect comparison. The accuser is an inner guide sought for in a wrong direction.

The accuser's credibility grows even when the person feels that the distance to Self grows, and he feels bad about it. The accuser's voice about his uselessness gets strength from it, since according to the comparison made by the accuser the reason to the unease is that the person isn't in accordance with the world's thought. The reason to the unease is the distance to the own will, but according to the world's thought it doesn't exist. Therefore the reason according to the world's thought is the distance to the world's thought.

This way the accuser is quite a trap. The person can't anything but admit that everything isn't going right and the accuser pushes lies upon him, which the person keeps since he has learned them and thinks that they are true. No matter how much he would try to correct his condition based on the lies, his condition does not in fact improve, since he tries to correct the wrong problem.

The inner accuser that Alkuajatus means is equal to the outer guide in a situation, where the person hasn't yet abandoned his own inner will.

The outer guide means all the thoughts that distance one from Self. They are thoughts the person has copied from his environment, and thoughts the environment offers to the person in each moment.

The outer guide isn't a person anymore than the inner guide. In both cases it is a question of a function that is built out of thoughts, own or foreign. The purpose of one is to grow the distance to Self, and the purpose of the other one is to reduce the distance to Self.

The outer guide and accuser

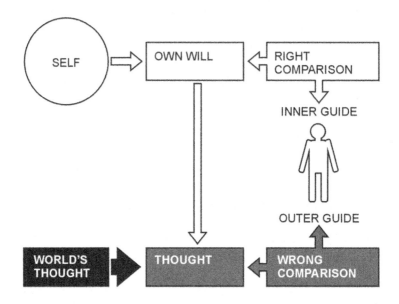

The picture shows how the inner guide changes into an outer guide. It happens by that the person performs a wrong comparison, in other words he compares his person with a thought formed by the world's thought.

The person experiences the outer guide to be accusatory, if he still has an existing connection to his own will. If he abandons his own will and takes up the world's thought, he doesn't experience the accusation produced by the wrong comparison, since he no longer experiences a conflict.

The accusing voice is the voice of the conflict between the own will and the world's thought, and which comes from the direction of the world's thought. It expresses the world's thought's estimation of the person, as the person himself experiences it.

The person experiences relief by that his conflict compared to the taught knowledge decreases, if his connection to Self and the own will weakens. Then the consciousness of the distance between the own will and the fulfilled life is weak, and the untruthful purpose of life is stronger.

If his connection to Self is strong, he doesn't experience any relief by correcting his person based on the lies, since the real problem doesn't get corrected by that, rather it gets worse.

He can get rid of the self-accusations to the extent he manages to reveal the world's lie to himself and confirm to himself that matters he internally knows to be true, are true.

For one who has a weak connection to Self it is possible to reduce this conflict by strengthening the unanimity about that the lies are true. He needs to accept the world's thought as the life controlling factor instead the own thought.

He will although imagine that he has his own thought even then, but what he has is a modification of the world's thought, built on the learned valuations and conceptions of life. He is therefore an artificial person, who not in any respect is an independent or a free person. The viewpoint of experiencing the own will is then in the wrong place, in other words it is not in the real viewpoint of the own will.

The accuser produces pain only to those, who still have a remaining connection to Self. The greater attraction towards the truth they experience, the stronger the accuser reacts. It even rewards a complete joining with the world's thought.

The existing help, that is recognized by the world, to correct the inner condition is based on the try to seek the solution in adaptation to the artificial person, since only that serves the world's thought, and no other thoughts are recognized.

The accuser, in other words the outer guide, is an untruthful thought model, unlike the original guiding function. All lies are thoughts, which are used to cover the connection to Self. This lie, as well as other lies, the person has himself built in his own mind, and he can also disassemble it himself.

What is here called the accuser can be realized in many ways. It can be self-accusations, it can be depreciation of the own person, it can be any submitted attitude towards the surrounding world.

It can be thought of as an independent being, as some even experience it, but it is still just a collection of thoughts, which the person uses to criticize himself when performing a comparison regarding his life.

The inner guide could be thought of as a compass in life, and the accuser as a magnet placed next to it, and which distorts the direction given by the compass.

Its misleading force is used in the religions, governments, trade and everything else where there is an intention to have an influence on the direction the person should move in. As a fact still remains, that all other sources who define the person's direction instead of his original own will are lies and misguidance.

The simplest way to oppose the accuser is not to believe it. Its strength is in its acceptance. If one doesn't listen to it, it starts to weaken. Not listening to it might cause pain, but the pain starts to weaken to the same extent as its strength. The same thing works on it that works on all lies, in other words every lie that has been seen through ceases to have effect. As well as the lie has been revealed to oneself, as well it disappears along with its influence.

Stray paths of the seeker

The connection to the real Self and the true own will is in the present world something that is hard to reach. Therefore even an honest seeker can build up illusions of what the own will and Self means.

The seekers path can be very long. It is always longer than what the person wishes it would be. Therefore it easily happens that the person wants to imagine to have reached his own will, even if he still is far away from it.

The imaginary reaching is a trap produced by the images built in the artificial person's viewpoint, where it is convenient for the person to imagine to have reached something he hasn't reached. It is a question of impatience that tempts one into self-deception.

Due to the images about spiritual reality, the truth, and good and bad offered by the world, the person can get lost inside a world of thought-images, where he tries to play the role of a good and pure person in accordance with the valuations of the world's thought.

Many who have chosen the spiritual path have ended up at this, and try to guide others to goodness in accordance with their illusions, and some of them even enjoy their show.

The surrounding world might confirm their good thoughts to them, and this way the person gets support for his illusions. However, no one is helped by beautiful pictures that ultimately are in the viewpoint of the world's thought. Nobody's inner freedom grows as a consequence of that, and no one approaches his true self.

The trap of beautiful pictures is built out of thought-images that are used to define the truth. As long and to the extent the person himself believes the illusions to be true, he will use them as his base of comparison in relation to his life and actions. He might feel good, even if the base of comparison is incorrect.

Also such a person who is well on the way to approaching Self and the own will might fall into the imagined own will, which is from the artificial person's viewpoint experienced will. The will that is experienced in the artificial person's viewpoint is never own real will. It is always against the own will.

Reaching the own real will is accomplished by that the person starts approaching his own will from the level of error, in other words the distance where he is when he begins. When he continues the approaching, the error in relation to the own will decreases constantly.

If the person at some point encounters some matter, in other words a lie, he absolutely doesn't want to abandon, then he ceases to approach the own will and moves to the artificial person's viewpoint to protect what he doesn't want to abandon. Then he remains on that distance from the own will, and can't make any progress before he performs the abandonment of the lie.

Gradually the condition of his own will starts to get weaker and the artificial person's viewpoint starts to grow stronger. A prolonged weakening of the condition eventually leads to that he most likely no longer is capable of reaching his own real will fully during his lifetime.

The one who is astray explains to himself that his errors are right, and he experiences his condition in accordance to it, if he manages to cover the consciousness of that it isn't.

The only existing antidote for that is honesty to oneself. The person himself knows his condition, if he is honest to himself.

Distances

Distance table

TRUTH - The person can see the matter clearly. This is the practical truth.

CONFRONT - The person is capable of looking at the matter and approaching it.

ANGER - The person rises up above the lies and makes an effort to clarify them

SUBMIT - The person gives up, that is submit, even thought he knows it is wrong.

FORGET - With time the person lets the matter sink into oblivion, he doesn't want to take responsibility.

LIE - The matter has sunk into oblivion, it no longer comes into mind. For the person it doesn't exist.

In the picture above there is a distance table.

Distance means the person's condition compared to the wanted condition. The wanted condition is in accordance with his original own will, it is not an imagined will.

The person experiences his present condition and his wanted condition in accordance with his consciousness. He can experience it strongly from the viewpoint of the world's thought or when he is on a higher level of consciousness, he experiences it from a viewpoint that is closer to Self.

The distance between the person's real condition and real will appears to the extent the person is aware of them. A condition that has been defined this way is the only completely truthful definition of the person's condition.

The consciousness covers at its full width even areas that the person can't see, but he might feel their existence and they influence him.

The person's experience of his own condition is determined by the person's ability to confront his own condition and his own real will.

The closer he is to the truth about his condition, the more stable he approaches the awareness of Self.

If the person's perception of his own condition to a large extent is confused by the artificial person's viewpoint, then his movement is unstable and his perception of the own condition is changeable.

If the person sufficiently strengthens the artificial person, defines his will in accordance with the world's thought and forgets his own will, then his movement towards a permanent artificial person is stable.

The distance appears in practice as the person's state of mind in relation to the matter when he focuses his attention to it. If he doesn't focus his attention to it, then it doesn't influence in any way. His attention is focused on it to the extent it is related to something he is doing, or experiences that he should do. The attention might be the product of a conscious choice, but it might as well be brought up to the consciousness by the situation, or a feeling brought up by an internally experienced need.

The distance table can be used to measure the person's distance to any matter within the frames of his own will or compared to it. The person's state of emotion reflects his average distance to the matters he is aware of, or what he believes them to be.

The closer the person is to the artificial person, the more the perceived is based on imagining, and is not actual consciousness, but distances between thoughts that are built on lies.

The relation between the will and the present condition can be measured only in individual matters, since each matter has its own distance to the will in the person's consciousness. With their sum the general condition can be described to the extent all possible distances have been measured. In practice such isn't possible, but evaluations can be made of the person's emotional state.

One must be careful when evaluating the emotional state, since some current problem or feeling of happiness can influence the person strongly at that moment, and it doesn't describe his general condition. This definition can be of help to a guide, but otherwise the defining of emotional states is completely unnecessary and could even be harmful.

Most useful the evaluating is in everyone's own use, when everyone can themselves follow their person, and learn to understand how their person functions. This understanding the person can use to his benefit when he is striving to grow his consciousness, and when revealing to himself the lies he has in his mind, which prevent him from seeing the truth.

The condition the person should be in according to his own will changes constantly. Will isn't stationary, it is movement. When the person reaches the sufficient level of truth, in other words the matters' relation to the own will is the sufficient truth, he is in the truth as long as the level in question is adequate.

When the requirement level rises, his distance from the sufficient truth grows, since the level of sufficient truth rises. The person's relation to the new level starts at the bottom of the table.

Before the new requirement level is topical, there is no relation to it, in other words it is in the lie. That level of truth doesn't exist to the person in that moment. When there appears a need for it, it begins to rise into the mind, in other words the person's distance compared to it is in the section "forget" in the table. When the person approaches it, it rises from the bottom of the table to the top of the table, where the person's relation to it is the truth.

Distance – Truth

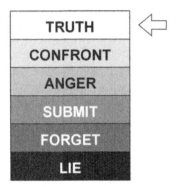

The truth is the practical truth, in other words it is the truth on the level the person's own will requires. The truth defined by the own will is equal to the sufficient level of truth, in other words the practical truth. It is completely true on its own level, it is not an opinion, and it doesn't differ from the absolute truth in other than its accuracy.

The requirement level considering the truth defined by the own will can't be changed, it is what it is. Not any opinion, wish or believable explanation makes it something else.

The truth is very absolute, completely black and white and without conditions.

The person is either able to see the matter clearly or then he doesn't see it completely clearly. It is true only when it is fully clear. The slightest inaccuracy compared to the requirement level makes in insufficient, since it isn't true enough. Then the person isn't in the truth, since he isn't finished with the confrontation.

One has to be thorough and patient when reaching for the truth, and to listen to the inside on a very fine tuned level for it to really clear up. If it doesn't become fully clear, it hasn't been reached and becomes a problem later on.

While reaching for the truth, a human trait is to try proving to oneself, that what has been reached is sufficiently true. Then it easily happens so that the person doesn't want to notice the places that aren't sufficiently true.

It is good to question the own understanding, however much one believes it to be good enough. We have to remember, that what is sufficiently true withstands questioning. Only lies are in danger there.

One of the most usual obstacles for insight of the truth is that the person strives towards a suitable truth that he has decided in advance, and that is based on the wishes he maintains. It is good to understand, that one can't reach the truth with a lie under the arm. This isn't affected by if the person is aware of his lies or not.

Searching for the truth is capitulation to Self and abandonment of the lies. Self constantly knows the complete truth, and therefore it is never a question of that Self wouldn't know, but always that the person's consciousness is limited, and the search for the truth is the disassembling of this limitation.

When in the truth, the person is in complete balance and harmony in relation to the matter, since his inner guide tells him that he is in his own will.

Distance – Confront

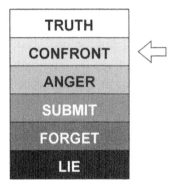

To confront means that the person insistently looks at a matter he already recognizes until he sees it fully, in other words completely clearly. When this has happened, he moves to the truth in relation to it. The confrontation hasn't been fully completed until the matter has been seen through thoroughly.

It is easy for the human to think that confrontation is inconvenient, and there is a great risk that he leaves the confrontation half done by lying to himself he already knows, in other words that he has already moved to the truth regarding the matter.

One who patiently confronts matters will notice that after every insight one can find even more in it. The confrontation isn't completed after the first insight, but it proceeds layer by layer.

For the result to be what is required for the understanding of the sufficient truth, the matter needs to be observed very patiently and for so long, that it really has become clear.

The truth doesn't reward speed, it only rewards the good understanding of the matter.

Distance – Anger

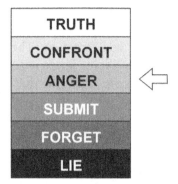

Anger is to create pressure toward the matter in order to get a breakthrough. When the person is able to get angry, he can raise the state of his consciousness enough to be able to start the confrontation.

To be able to focus the anger correctly, the person's consciousness in relation to the matter has to be mature enough, so that he can push himself up to the level of confrontation. A correctly focused anger directs its strength on the unclearness in his mind, and never on the environment.

Before the anger, the person isn't capable of recognizing the problem accurately. The anger is a flow, with which Self raises its person's consciousness enough for him to be able to find the right target.

An incorrectly directed anger is a try, in a too weak state of consciousness, to correct a problem that is in the borderlines of submission. The anger must be directed correctly to be of corresponding benefit.

The best way to focus the anger is simply done by not pushing forcibly, but to observe the matter and wait for it to rise by itself. It will rise up when the time is right, if the person has will in the matter. A small attempt to raise it might be useful. One can dip the toe in the water, but one mustn't make the mistake to force it.

When the anger starts rising up naturally, one mustn't try to stop it, since it is the route to the beginning of confrontation. The anger is sometimes strong and sometimes very slight. There is no rule for its strength, and one mustn't try to make it into something else than what it is.

Suppressing the anger might be harmful, a small exaggeration isn't. The suppressing of it stops the movement, and the person won't move to the confrontation, but remains in place in the matter. He prevents himself from solving the problem.

When the person is ready for anger, but doesn't complete it, he might fall back into submission or be caught in anger that hasn't been completed. Incomplete angers can accumulate to a pressure that is left as an explosive accumulation of emotions in the mind.

If the person experiences enough pressure, this explosive accumulation could produce a furious anger, but it is a confused outburst that doesn't solve any problems, since it is not clearly focused on anything. It might bring relief, but it doesn't get solved since it lacks order.

The burden that is born out of unfinished efforts is solved by that the person gets one matter at a time in motion, and moved to confrontation.

The other alternative to be released from the burden is to get the person to through forgetting lower the matters into lie, in which case they cease to trouble him. This however, can't be considered to be a solution, since it is preventing of the own person and supporting of the artificial person. Neither does the problem get solved, it is only hidden.

The person's strive is to raise each matter up to the truth, and the own will doesn't have giving up as an alternative. If the world's thought, which the person has adopted, causes strong pressure to prevent the own will from rising, the person can be prevented from the confronting of matters even very completely, and a consequence of that might be even a strong pressure of prevented anger.

A person who doesn't yield to the world's thought, in other words who refuses to forget himself, but neither lifts the matters up to confrontation and eventually to the truth, is easily caught in a trap where there are matters caught in anger as well as submission.

Distance – Submit

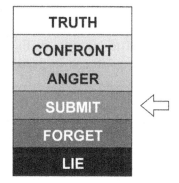

Submission happens when the person into his mind accepts a thought, that is a lie compared to the need of the own original will. He decreases his consciousness of the truth in favor of the lie. Every accepting of a lie produces distance compared to the own will, and accepting lies is to submit whether the person is aware of it or not.

Submission happens a lot as a child, when the child with starry eyes accepts everything the adult world teaches. Unfortunately the world teaches the world's thought and completely forgets to leave space for the child's own person, since it according to the world's thought doesn't exist.

Seen from the child's viewpoint the submission hardly feels at all, since the child's first task is to create the viewpoint for life for himself, from which he later begins to create his own life. He can't learn a thought, or a way of thinking, that the world doesn't have to offer. Neither can he create himself space that the world isn't offering. Therefore he has to create the starting viewpoint for his own life out of the material that is at hand.

Another thing, seen from the child's viewpoint, that reduces the feeling caused by the growth of the distance, is that the child at that point doesn't have to fulfill his own will, but only to create the foundations for his coming life. Therefore the errors have no influence, from his viewpoint seen.

They start to influence later, in youth. Then he hardly remembers his own will, but the better he has managed to preserve it, the stronger he experiences the distance to his own will and its needs that was created in his childhood.

People submit themselves to many things during their lives, when they lack the strength to start opposing the pressure from the environment. Pressure from the environment is, among other things, other people's attitudes and desire to decide what everyone should be and how.

A strong pressure is represented by the society's demands, which are based on the force of hierarchical power. The strongest measures to subject are the wars, where a large numbers of people are forced to accept the thought of someone else under the threat of death.

People are subjected with religions by offering the imaginary world of the religions to control their lives. Religious communities can be very powerful subjugators. The most significant subjecting force isn't in their way of life or their other demands. The strongest subjecting is the lie that shuts out the inner world, with which the person is prevented from a connection to Self and his own original will.

When the person has some matter on the level of submission, he experiences piteousness and powerlessness. He might be tired and experience different emotions of weakness. He who strives upwards from submission has to succeed in rising to anger, where he creates a pressure that will institute the solution of the problem.

To create anger, he has to for some time confront the dullness of the submitted condition. When he begins to approach anger in the matter, the pain he experiences of it grows. The strength of the pain depends on the matter. The harder it is to confront, the more pain he can expect before he is capable of creating anger, with which he rises above the pain.

In submission the person is underneath that limit of pain, and when he rises to anger, he is above that pain. The pain has the same magnitude at the turning point, but when in anger, he rises to control the pain and it is an easier viewpoint than the submitted condition, where the pain controls the person. After a while the pain begins to ease, when the person approaches the ability to begin the confronting of the matter.

Very usually the world's thought offers withdrawal and giving up as the solution to the person's problems, in other words it offers submission to ease the pain. The pain will ease if the person manages to move his person to the level of forgetting, where the matter begins to pass out of mind.

Distance – Forget

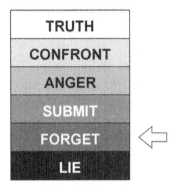

When the submission continues, the person gives up and begins to forget what was true. The lie starts to replace the truth as a point of reference.

Forgetting is the voluntary lowering of the consciousness.

Forgetting is in fact self-deception, where the matter is permanently pushed out of sight, so that it wouldn't be present reminding of its existence. The person moves his viewpoint away from the truth completely, so that the truth wouldn't disturb his life.

Many recommend that one should forget painful memories, and it is even defined as the normal functioning of the mind, with which the own person is protected. This interpretation of the mind's functioning is probably based on the discovery, that people very usually do precisely so.

The memories are painful until they are confronted, and clarity in them is obtained. When clarity in them is obtained, in other words they are freed from the influence of lies, the pain ceases and the consciousness is freed.

The cause of pain regarding painful memories is the performing of wrong comparisons. When the matter is pushed out of mind, one tries to avoid the trouble of revealing the lies related to the matter, and seeks peace of mind in lowering the consciousness.

When some matter rises up from the lie, then this level of unconsciousness is the returning into mind. Then the person begins to experience mild pain, since the awareness of the distance to the truth begins to rise up.

When he this way becomes more aware of the matter that is rising up, he can accelerate the returning into mind by listening to himself very carefully, and by observing the slightly visible matter.

Distance – Lie

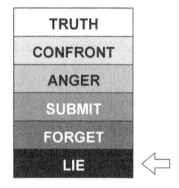

Lie is a state of unconsciousness.

Lie is a condition where the person lacks the truth, that the own will requires, about the matter.

For the matter to be in lie, the matter in question needs to be one that should be in the person's consciousness, but it is in unconsciousness.

Lie is a condition where the person's relation to the matter is in full balance, since he doesn't hear his inner guide, and the matter in question isn't at all a point of reference.

For there to be a conflict, the matter needs to rise up to the consciousness through the level of forgetting when it gradually begins to come into the mind. On the level of forgetting it begins to produce a slight conflict, since the voice of the inner guide begins to be heard weakly, and it brings forth the conflict between the present condition and the own real will.

In lie, in unconsciousness, there are also matters that shouldn't be in the person's consciousness, since they are not topical to him. Those matters have no relation to the person that would in any way affect him, since they don't belong within the frames of the person's will in that moment.

They are practical lies, with which the expedient finiteness is maintained. Therefore they are not taken into account in the distances that have an influence on the person's condition, and that regard the person's relation to matters that should be in his consciousness.

The states of life

Meaning of the diagrams

The diagrams in this chapter present how many matters the person has on each distance from the truth. Each matter is on some distance, and these diagrams illustrate the person's general state.

Since the person's consciousness of his own state can be weak, and he might even compare his state to wrong things, the person's realized states of emotion aren't a confident indicator for his distance from the truth.

Mankind's consciousness of the own will is so weak, that the major part of people are in fact in an untruthful state, or even in a weaker state than that.

The nature of the states is marked on the left side of the diagram. The states of truth are states that serve the truth, in other words the top three states. The states of lie are the bottom three states, since their pressure serves the lie.

On the top and the bottom of the right side there is balance. The balance is caused by that a matter that is in the truth, as well as a matter that is in the lie, isn't in conflict with anything.

In the intermediate states there is pain and unbalance. Between submission and anger is the strongest point of pain and confusion. When moving up or down from that point, the pain and confusion decreases.

When matters rise into consciousness, the person's general state might get weaker as the sum of all matters, but it is a phenomenon that is related to the moment in question, and it is not decreasing of his level.

No state is permanent. With the own will is associated a continuous rise of consciousness, and therefore each and everyone even in a free state must take care of the continuous needs of the progress. In other case their state begins to weaken in relation to the purpose.

Balanced state

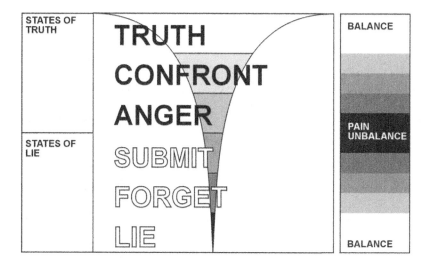

In this diagram the person has most part of the matters, which are related to his own will, in the truth. He is balanced and he lifts with a steady pace matters from the unconsciousness, and processes them with a sufficient speed.

The prerequisite for progress is the continuous rise of matters from the unconsciousness, in other words from the lie. When matters rise from the unconsciousness with a steady pace and they are processed with sufficient speed, the balance is preserved.

In the world a state that resembles this is fulfilled for many people in such a way, that the point of reference isn't the own real will, but the artificial person's will in accordance with the world's thought.

This state, as the true one, is the goal of everyone. In this state the person is free.

Hauling state

The person in this diagram has quite many of all matters in the truth, but he is behind with the confrontation of matters. Therefore his movement isn't very free and his state is somewhat instable.

The person's consciousness is on a good level. He needs to work on matters diligently, and his pain will decrease and his clearness will grow.

Working on matters is to acquire knowledge, to observe it and to reveal lies. It is also the observation of the own inside and the growing the level of consciousness in matters. The truth will set one free, nothing else will.

Heavy state

When the person has a lot of matters that he is aware of but hasn't cleared them, in other words lifted them to the truth, his movement is slow and his life is troublesome. His state is heavy in relation to the own will. He has a lot of pain and unbalance.

The person's consciousness is strong, but a forceful confusion and pain is a heavy burden on him. The solution is to confront matters with the best possible speed, whereby each matter will rise towards the truth.

In the same way as in the hauling state, the person is freed by acquiring knowledge, observing it and his inner world.

Untruthful state

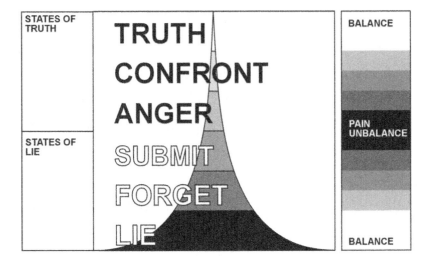

In this diagram the person's relation to the own will is mostly in the unconsciousness. Since he isn't aware of his distance, he doesn't experience pain of it. His balance is quite good, but he is slightly aware of that something is missing in life. He can experience it as a hollow feeling inside him.

For a person who lives steadily in the world's thought, the state in relation to the own will is an even weaker state than this one. In that state almost all matters in relation to the own will are in the lie, or perhaps slightly above it.

If the person begins to raise his consciousness in this state, he will pass through the heavy state and the hauling state before his consciousness is really freed. Seemingly his state will degrade, since a lot of matters, that won't clear for a long time, will come into the consciousness.

The guides of Alkuajatus won't strive to help a person in this state, if not a particularly strong will rises from the person himself.

Natural development

Natural or normal development.

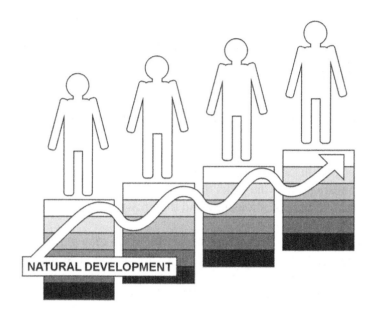

When the person has reached his starting level, in other words the level of truth required by the own will, from where the free movement of the own will can be fulfilled, the person's development will continue towards a higher consciousness with a normal pace. Before that the most central matter was to reach the freeing of the own will. From that point on, the development is a part that is related to the fulfilling of the own will.

The natural development progresses in a wavelike fashion upwards. When the person reaches some level all the way to the truth, he begins to get aware of the next one. The consciousness of the next level rises, since the movement of the own will requires the raising of the level.

It has a lowering influence on his general state since something, that isn't clear to the person at that stage, begins to rise up into the consciousness.

When the person clears the new level thoroughly, he is again in the truth in relation to the requirement of his own will, and after some time the consciousness required by the new level starts to come into mind.

This way the movement is wavy, where each peak is above the previous one, and every new base is higher up than the earlier one.

The arrow in the picture illustrates the wavy growth of the consciousness, and the steps that show the distances illustrate the clearness of the consciousness and the growth of that level.

In the picture, the person sinks from the truth to anger, and from there he rises back to the truth. It is not a rule. The sinking of clearness can be strong as well as it can be unnoticeable. The picture only illustrates the principle of the wavy movement.

There can also be big time differences in how fast the person manages to reach a new level. Many factors influence the time used, and the first and most significant factor is the requirement of the own will. Without it there is no need in that moment, and therefore nothing happens.

It is good to remember, that it is not a question of a race in the growth of consciousness, but it is a question of being in honest compliance with the own will.

Levels of truth and consciousness

Personal level of truth

The level of truth means the distance of the knowledge from the absolute truth. The closer the person is to the absolute truth, the higher level of truth he is on.

The person's level of truth is his own will's level of truth. It is that whether he has cleared the area or not. The clearer his relation to himself is, the clearer he is also his own person and on his own level of truth.

The own will's level of truth is the natural level of the person when he is creating his own person. He can lower his person's level of consciousness by starting to act a role that is lower than his own level of truth.

In other words, the person has a personal level of truth already at birth. He observes the world and his inner world from that viewpoint. All lies that prevent him from seeing clearly weaken him and cause him pain.

He can raise the level of truth only after he has cleared and freed his starting level. The starting level means the level that is the required level for the free fulfilling of the own will. It is his level of truth at his birth.

Before that level is cleared, his level of truth is on its starting level, and he must clear it completely before he is fully ready to move in accordance with his own will. The possible changes of level from that on are matters of the need defined by the own will.

The person's ability is strongly tied to the viewpoint defined by his own will. The higher it is compared to the average viewpoint of the world, the more capable he is and the greater his conflict is in relation to the world. And the less he agrees to forget his original will, the more this conflict causes him pain.

If one forgets himself and changes completely into an artificial person, then life is painless. It is in fact not fully possible, since one can't abandon himself, even if the consciousness can be lowered, and therefore some degree of consciousness is preserved in any case. It might rise up some day and cause the collapse of the person's world.

Another alternative to reach painlessness is to do all the required work to clear the mind so that the own original will's level of truth is fully reached.

A complete painlessness can never be reached, since all development requires opening of the consciousness, and a consequence of that is some degree of pain. When the person's inner condition is cleared to his starting level, the pain from that on is very mild. It could be called the normal condition.

Levels of truth

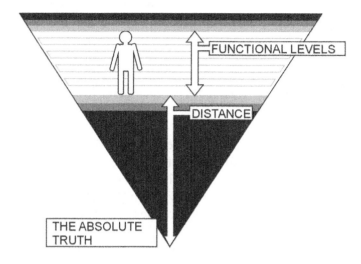

The level of truth is the level of inner consciousness on some distance from the absolute truth. The levels are imaginary, since there doesn't exist actual levels, however, there exist distances.

The level of truth is functional and fully reached when the person's relation to it is clear, in other words he sees it completely clearly.

On the functional levels, the person's movement is free and he is capable to the extent of the levels height and clearness.

In the picture above, the levels of truth are illustrated by the white levels. Both above and below them are gray and black levels. The gray levels are in the consciousness, but are unclear. The black levels are in the unconsciousness.

There is unconsciousness on both sides. The levels which the person hasn't yet focused on are unclear to him, or then he isn't even aware of them.

The level of truth is a viewpoint. There exist lower viewpoints and higher viewpoints, in relation to which the person's consciousness is weak, or then there is no relation.

The person is capable of communication and other activity on the levels he is aware of. It happens on each level with the clarity he has on the level in question.

Confronting of lower levels is necessary only when there for some reason is a need to specify the nature of them to oneself. For instance, to be able to help a person whose level of consciousness is on a lower level, one must be capable of understanding the level of consciousness, on which that helped person is.

The complete understanding of lover levels requires going to those viewpoints, and rising out of them by revealing their lies.

Getting upwards requires the raising of the own consciousness, which is the opening of one's own inner state of unconsciousness.

Consciousness

Consciousness is to be aware of a level of truth.

Consciousness is also clarity in relation to some level of consciousness.

When the person clarifies his own personal level of truth, his consciousness clears in relation to that level of truth.

When he raises his level of truth and clarifies it, his consciousness clears similarly, only on a new level.

Helping levels to raise the consciousness

IMPOSSIBLE LEVEL FOR THE TARGET	
TOO DIFFICULT LEVEL FOR THE TARGET	
HELPS TO INSIGHT	
STRENGHTENS THE LEVEL OF THE TARGET	LEVEL OF THE TARGET PERSON
WEAKENS THE TARGET	

For helping one must be able to choose the appropriate level of helping.

Level of helping is the level of clarity compared to something.

Helping in this context is to help the person to clarify his own inner world to himself. Helping is the clarifying of knowledge so that the unclearness, in other words the lie, breaks down.

If the target is provided with knowledge that is too far away from his condition in that moment, he can't get anything useful out of it. In other words it doesn't help him at all.

When he is provided with knowledge in a form he barely can reach, it is heavy and difficult to him. He is helped with it, but in a very hard way.

The appropriate level is one where the person manages to use the provided knowledge with a reasonable effort, and can that way raise his clarity in the matter.

If we discuss with the person on the level he is on, it strengthens his ties to the level in question.

Knowledge on a lower level, on the other hand, frustrates the person and strives to pull him downwards. In other words it weakens the person's condition.

The balance of the consciousness

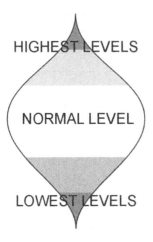

When the person's consciousness is on its normal level, in other words on his own personal level of truth, his consciousness in relation to different matters is divided in accordance with the picture above.

His normal level is clear and bright. The highest levels, which lead to development, are unclear but he clarifies them. He is to some extent capable of activity on his own top level.

He has matters also on the lower levels. He clarifies also those, as it is topical.

The higher levels have to be clarified for there to be development. The lower levels have to be clarified, so that they don't become a burden for the raising of consciousness.

The lower levels could be considered to be his weaknesses, but as long as they don't pull him downwards, they belong to the normal condition. If the person is very worried about the matters, where his consciousness is weaker, his attention goes too much to them and it weakens the development.

He doesn't have to worry about anything else but that the matters on the lower levels don't fall too much behind the overall.

Likewise, if the person's attention is only on the areas of his highest levels, he will weaken his development by neglecting the taking care of the overall.

When considering the overall, the normal level is meant for the major activity. The tops and the weakest points take only a minor part in the activity.

The balance of the consciousness is a matter that should be taken care of, since that best serves the own will and its progress.

The growth of society's consciousness

On the societal level, the personal levels of truth are divided in such a way, that there are a few higher tops, a lot of mediocrity and a few with weaker consciousness. One must notice that the issue here isn't societal positions, but levels of consciousness.

For the society to be able to develop in the direction of the own wills, it has to reach a sufficient clearness on the different levels of truth of the entirety.

Alkuajatus must be provided to all levels in accordance with the possibilities. If it is provided only to some level, the growth of clarity will slow down, since the consciousness of the persons on each level must be freed for the entirety to work.

The weaker the clearness is on the lower levels, the harder it is for the middle level and especially the top level to be freed to full functioning. If the middle level, in proportion, clarifies more than the top, then the middle level will need the top's help to progress more than the top is capable of providing.

The law of helping doesn't function if some level is over- or underrepresented. The functionality of the entirety is then weak and unbalanced, in other words the balance of the consciousness of the entirety isn't in order.

To be able to fulfill Alkuajatus in the world, it must be provided to everyone and everywhere. The tops are the guides for the middle levels, and the middle levels guide those on the weaker levels. Everyone is needed, as long as everyone delivers the thing they have come here to do.

At the moment the need of guiding is the greatest need, since the lack of it prevents all.

The greatest task of guiding in this moment is to help to grow the clarity of the existing level of truth, in other words to help clarifying the starting level of the own wills.

The inner reality is the home of the consciousness

The inner reality is the home of the consciousness. It is the most central matter to each and everyone, but it is tried to bypass, since it doesn't serve the goals of the hierarchical power system.

The inner reality isn't valued in this world. The attitude towards it is as if it didn't have any significance and as if the outer reality would be the base of all real.

This attitude grows the appreciation of materiality and makes the inner reality a subject of materiality. In the order of precedence the material things come first and the inner reality is noticed only if it causes a lot of trouble.

The human is raised up to take care of the material world primarily and the inner reality is considered to be a side issue.

When problems emerge, the attention is on the fulfillment of the outer order, not on the clarifying of the inner reality. The goal is to subject one to the image of reality offered by the world's thought, not the growth of the inner freedom.

This way the person's self-experience is tried to tie to the image of reality of the world's thought, and the goal is to help him to order in accordance with that thought. By this the consciousness is trapped inside the boundaries set by outer power.

If the person learns to deal with his life correctly in accordance with those thoughts, he is seen from the viewpoint of the world's thought to be in a good condition. He has bowed to forget himself and is content with using the taught and accepted thoughts in the creating of his life.

His reward is outer approval. His loss is inner emptiness.

This is the way the world functions, even though the inner reality is where life is experienced and from where it is created, and its freedom is the most central matter in life.

Guiding

Guiding is the highest form of help

Guiding in this context is to guide some person to find himself and towards his own person.

The guide's task is to help the guided to gradually find his inner guide. The guide is the help that compensates the lack of the inner guide.

Helping is to help the approaching of Self. It is an activity that helps the growth of the own person and supports the clarifying of the own will. In life, a correctly functioning fulfilling of the own will is always the helping of others.

Guiding is the most pure helping of Self and the own will. It is very demanding and it requires a very high responsibility for the own person and the ability to provide knowledge.

A true guide is a guide in every moment. He is that from birth, it is his self-evident purpose of life. He is ready to walk the entire difficult route that eventually leads to that he can do what he came here to do.

The route is difficult and it requires a constant growth of inner honesty, which often is to perform very difficult abandonment. He will abandon everything to the very point where there is nothing left, since only from that level can his actual life begin.

He is interested in finding the truth at any cost and he is interested in helping those he guides in a very relentless way. He must have a good ability to confront anything.

A guide is a person, whose own original will is precisely that.

A guide will always remain in clarity to the best of his ability, he doesn't bow to anything to please people. He represents the route to the truth, and he will bring forth that route without hesitation. His only purpose is to help others in finding it.

A guide gives time to those who want it, and a true guide will without trouble leave without time the persons, who don't really want it. The guided doesn't control the guiding. The guide guides, he doesn't drag anyone along. The guided must do his journey himself.

A person who wants is one who is ready to work to reach clarity and is very interested in clarifying himself to himself, and in abandoning the world's thought by revealing its lies.

One who doesn't have true will to find himself, wants to discuss and spend time in pleasant company, and doesn't want to confront himself or work in order to grow his clarity. Instead he wants to maintain the world's thought in his life, and demands that others accept it as the base for existence. When the question of taking responsibility for oneself is raised, he comes up with reasons why he isn't ready for it. All reasons are reflections of fear, none of them are true.

One who is untruthfully interested of being guided holds on to the world's thought tightly, since he is afraid to start abandoning it. He doesn't strive in the direction of the own will and Self. He wants to drag the guide in the direction of the world's thought.

Naturally those who show no will in finding themselves are those the guide shouldn't waste his time on, since that time can be usefully used where the guiding gives results.

These same things apply in all human relations. It is always a question of taking responsibility in everything, and the taking of responsibility begins with the own person. A person who doesn't want to put an effort into finding his own real self, nor into creating a person in accordance with his own will, lives in lie.

The one who lives in lie isn't helped by understanding that accepts stagnancy or movement downwards. This kind of understanding pulls down the helped, as well as the guide.

Then the goal of the guided is not to rise up, but to pull the guide down to the world's thought. This accepting is submission and the growth of lie for both parts. The guide loses his ability to guide even himself, and the guided gets support for the sinking into lie.

The best choice the guide can make in that case is to really understand the situation and withdraw from it. Then the guide restores his ability to guide, and the guided at least has a chance to someday begin to confront the problems of his real selfhood.

A guided who wants to ask questions without any other strive besides to rotate confused images in his thoughts, wants to avoid the confrontation of matters. He is afraid of that.

A guided who strives to argue about the matter and demands evidence is trying to defend his existing perception, and isn't truly willing to study the matter and taking the responsibility for its confrontation.

A guided who demands that the guiding should be something he understands to be the right way for him, doesn't really want to confront matters, but wants company on his own level.

A guided who sets terms and conditions for the route, and for what the truth can look like, doesn't want to find the truth, he only wants to find something to confirm his existing set of values.

There are countless alternatives, but common for all of them is the unwillingness to confront and a try to get acceptance for the own perceptions, which are thought-images that support the world's thought.

A reluctant guided doesn't need guiding. He is not going anywhere, but is only spinning around in circles and is confused in relation to the matter.

No one can get an insight for someone else, or want for someone else. If these aren't found in the person himself, nothing good will happen. The guided stays as a prisoner of the world's thought. The guide's purpose is not to help in adapting to the world's thought, since it is not the help it is a question of when guiding.

The guide doesn't save his energy when it comes to finding the right help for an honest guided. This help is the required knowledge and skill. He doesn't pity anyone, since it would be to lie. He is ready to help those who can be helped, and he is ready to leave those he can't help on the side of the road.

Guiding is a helping hand from the truth into the world of lies. The hand reaches out halfway. The other half is the problem of the guided. If the guided doesn't have will, the guide offers his hand to someone else.

The only meter when choosing who to help is the honesty and the will of the helped. If one or the other is missing, then there is nothing to be done to provide real help. Guiding is not a parlor game, or entertainment, it is concrete support for those who want to find themselves.

The only results of guiding are the insights, that moves the guided towards clarity and that will be visible in the behavior and the life of the guided. If clarifying doesn't occur, there has been no guiding, even if it has been tried. Everything else but the right results are explanations, that pave the way for the growth of the lie.

The guide must be able to tell the difference between true clarifying and the easing of the situation that is a consequence of the decreasing of pressure.

True clarifying is the clearing of knowledge and the consequent relief from that.

The decreasing of pressure that follows the easing of some situation makes the person feel better, but it contains no insight concerning Self. Then the eased feeling doesn't lead to the weakening of the world's thought, rather, the opposite can occur.

Without a real strive to insight of Self, the person will after the relief strive back to the world's thought, regardless if the relief is a consequence of clarifying the mind or the solving of a practical problem.

Depending on the condition of the guided, the results are slight or more visible, but they are not conspicuously absent.

If the guide isn't sufficiently clear in relation to himself and his goal, the confusion of the guided could easily begin to control the communication and events, and then the guide is no longer a guide, but is lost into the confusion of the guided.

The difference between a guide and others who are on the path of insights of selfhood, is that the guide is a full-time guide and his responsibility for the truth is high.

A human whose purpose of life is not to be a guide puts his effort, in accordance with his own will, in some other activity that helps the world, and which usually doesn't require an insight of self on the same level as for the guide. Nevertheless, he is helpful for those who seek the truth and might to some extent be a guide who helps one to get started.

The function of guiding

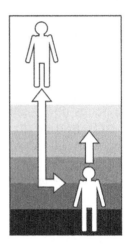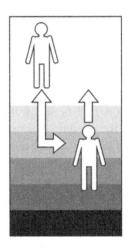

In the picture to the left, the guide is on the white area, which represents clearness of the consciousness, and he communicates with the guided who is on the black and gray areas, which represent unclearness.

There the communication works and is of good quality. The person gets uplift by the communication, and in the picture to the right he is rising towards a clearing consciousness.

While the guided is rising towards inner clearness, the guiding proceeds.

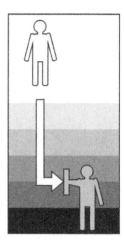 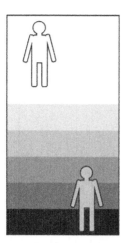

In this picture, the guide tries to communicate, but the guided refuses his communication. There can be many apparent reasons for the refusal, but it is always the refusal to look into matters such as they are. Then the person is defending his own artificial person.

On the right side the guide ceases to communicate and the guided is left where the guided started. The guide had to see the situation as such that the person didn't really want to begin the clarifying of his consciousness and begin to rise towards his real selfhood.

In a situation like this the guided might experience to have been abandoned if he has a will to rise, even if he fought against it.

It is difficult for the guided to see the uselessness of the situation from the guide's viewpoint, and it is also difficult for him to see his own refusal since the own refusal usually is clothed as, from the viewpoint of the guided, a reasonable attitude and matter.

Therefore it is difficult for the guided to understand that the guide is always there, the guide doesn't grow a distance, but the guided can do that.

No one can be abandoned but by his own choice. When he ceases to maintain the distance, he will notice that the distance didn't exist for any other reason.

To the left, the guided gets the control of the communication, in other words he succeeds in attracting the guide to the viewpoint of the world's thought's reality, and to observe matters from there. From this follows a downward pressuring influence on the guide.

On the right side the guide has lowered his consciousness and lost his touch to clearness in matters. The guided thinks that he has done a good deed, since his concept of reality has defeated the guide.

As a result the guide lost his ability to guide the guided, and also himself. He lost his clearness and decreased his consciousness.

A guided, who doesn't want to rise up, but gladly pulls the guide into the gentle arms of the world's thought, doesn't act by consciously thinking he is doing that. From his viewpoint seen his image of reality is truer, and in this case the guide fell for what the guided did offer as an inducement.

In that case the guide must distance himself from the situation and start focusing on what happened, and what made him to lose his viewpoint.

Helping

Helping

The helping needs to generate a profit.

Helping is an action that helps the fulfilling of the own will, regardless of who is the object of the helping.

The helper has to be capable of seeing the difference between the imagined will and the true will of the helped, so that real help can be provided.

Helping leads to the improvement of the condition of the helped in relation to the own will of the helped. If it doesn't lead to that, then it isn't helping, but the exploitation of the helper or the inability of the helper.

The helping must improve something in such way, that it leads to the improvement of the general condition, in other words it has to generate a profit in relation to the effort.

The law of spiritual nature

The law of spiritual nature means the conformity of law that prevails on the inner side. It is the life creating free will's normal state, which prevails when Self functions freely in its natural way.

Self always functions freely when its movement isn't distorted by any lie. It functions flawlessly on a level of truth in accordance with its will, and its influence on the material world begins with the creation of the life specific own will. This function's conformities of law apply on everyone, they are the common and natural basic principles for the actions of all beings.

The law of spiritual nature functions in relation to the material world when the being creates life. The law of spiritual nature functions outside of life with the same principle. In that context we could speak of bodiless beings, who act as correct as they are free. Bodilessness isn't freedom and not all the bodiless function flawlessly.

The law of helping

Helping is a law of the spiritual nature, and it is the basic structure in all existing. Helping is the building material for the stairs of development. Helping is reaching out with a hand to one, who wants to approach knowledge and consciousness. It is always at hand for one who has an honest will.

Helping isn't the duty of the helper, and being helped isn't a must. Both viewpoints are voluntary and their functionality requires will. Without will help can't be given, and the unwilling can't receive the help.

To find help

The law of helping would function freely and easily among mankind, if the humans would have a recognized right to the own free will and its inviolability. Then the human could grow up to be his own self from childhood, since the help of the upbringing would support the awareness of Self and the growth of the own will.

The law of helping works regardless of the ways of the world. Right now the getting of help requires more will and greater honesty, since the premises are weaker. Likewise, the helping is more difficult, since the own will and the relation to self of the helped is weak. The human's relation to the truth and the own self is so weak, that he is almost incapable of recognizing it.

With the strength of an honest will the person finds the answers that will open his consciousness, and he will find what he seeks. Good guiding makes possible what for the modern man is nearly impossible. But nothing is enough if the person's will isn't strong enough, and he isn't honest enough to himself.

When the will is strong and pure, the route to consciousness is found so that he finds the best possible route in one way or another. A pure will attracts the right solutions, which usually look like coincidences. It doesn't matter if the person doesn't know anyone who can guide him. He will find, or he will be found. The route exists, it is only a question of will and honesty.

The strength and honesty of the will are defined by the truth, they are not defined in accordance to what the person himself imagines them to be. The clearest indicator for the strength and the purity of the will is that the person finds precisely the answers he deserves. Deserving in this context is that he gets what he is willing or capable of receiving. In other words he is himself the one who defines what he eventually gets.

If the person imagines that his will is relentless and honest, but can't find the help for the right answers anywhere, the truth is that the strength and the purity of his will aren't sufficient. If they aren't sufficient, the person won't understand the right answers, even if they are right under his nose.

For the human it can be extremely difficult to understand how much will needs to be found, and how honest to oneself one must be. He who really wants always increases his effort, when he notices that is wasn't enough. He will increase it until it finally brings the result he was looking for.

It is good to be aware of that the result in accordance with the own will's requirement level can always be reached. The person can do nothing but win, if he doesn't give up.

Giving up is that oneself ceases to strive towards the own goal. The reason for giving up is that the person doesn't want to take responsibility for himself. He might think that it is too heavy or then he doesn't believe it is possible.

Behind all explanations the person can find submission to the common thinking, which means the thoughts among which he has been brought up, and which he principally has copied to be his ideas of life. It is always a question of a lie that the person himself holds on to.

The availability of help

The answers, which guide to levels of consciousness, that can't be found in this world require a very high level of will and honesty. Then the person finds pure answers inside himself by his own advice. This is, however, extremely exceptional and then it is a question of a renewal that aims to the raising of the world's level of consciousness.

It is so rare, that no one should in any case believe it to be in question. If someone insists that he is doing that, the only right decision the helper can make is to leave the person to his own devices, since the person in question can't be helped. If his claim would be true, he wouldn't need a helper, and a helper would only be of harm to him. If his claim isn't true, he either abandons that idea or is caught in it.

In this world one can find the answers, which some person has retrieved and confronted so well and so deep that he is able to give them a material form. Material existence is for instance writing or speech.

The answers are always on some specific level of truth. They are never the final answers of absolute truth. The answers are as correct as they purely represent the level of truth referred to. The real understanding of the answers requires a lot of will and a very good ability to be honest to oneself, and incredibly much patience.

The person's own will defines the level he seeks. He doesn't seek any other levels.

Let us notice, that no level of truth is complexity and a lot of fine words. It is nearness to the absolute truth, clearness and simplicity.

In all its simplicity it is hard to reach. Not so much because of that the understanding of the truth would be very difficult, but because the overcoming of the world's lie is very hard.

The law of helping in the spiritual world

The growth of consciousness requires guiding even in the spiritual world and the natural help there is always at hand.

In the spiritual world the law of helping prevails. There are no judgments, or power hierarchies, or power as many religions tend to describe it. There are levels of consciousness, and those on each level help those on the lower levels to find themselves and to carry out their own journey.

It is a route in accordance with the law of helping all the way to the absolute truth. It is not built with orders and forcing, nor punishments or judgments. It is built with free will and the law of helping.

The condition of help in the world

The structure of the world is at the moment based on hierarchical power. It bypasses the individual's own will, self and natural freedom. The premise of the power structure is the invented right to control individuals, which was made for the needs of power.

There the actions of the individuals are controlled by the centralistic thought, which isn't based on anyone's own will. That thought is built from the viewpoint of maintaining power, and it is to be formed from the viewpoint of preserving power. It is the compromise born out of one or another power struggle, and it is in fact not in anyone's interest, since only the free movement of the own real will is in each and everyone's interest. The centralistic thought deprives everyone's rights and possibilities to the own will's freedom.

The centralistic thought is a lie that has replaced the natural, free world's structure with power hierarchy. Its purpose is to help the strengthening and growth of the structures of power. Its purpose is not to provide help that promotes freedom. Therefore the guidance it offers can't properly speaking be called help, but rather a tool of power.

The hierarchical power is a way of thinking that has gradually been taught to the humans throughout the history of mankind, and at the present it is experienced to be so natural, that very few question it. Its alternative is seen to be arbitrary, in which nothing regulates the relations between people. Therefore it is experienced to be chaos that would ruin mankind.

The route that has lead to the accepting of centralistic power is a route of violence and forcing. It has not been born as a result of people's free wills, in other words it has no connection to the law of helping, to the law of spiritual nature.

Originally it was forcing and it still is that, even if very visible forcing isn't exercised. In many countries the forcing is visible, but in several countries its visibility is weak, since it has gradually been hidden into the upbringing in a way, where people submit themselves to its power mostly by accepting it.

The hierarchical power is experienced to be so natural that even those who oppose it, tries to overthrow the existing system by offering a new one in its place, which doesn't change the structures of power to anything else. They do this already for the reason that they don't want real freedom for people, but they want themselves to be the ones who define the system replacing the previous one.

A very popular system is the democratic model, where people by voting can decide who are going to form the centralistic thought. In democracies the freedom of people's own wills is to some extent wider than in other used alternatives.

Nevertheless, the own will's freedom is negligible, since even in those systems the responsibilities, options and actions are controlled with the centralistic thought, that subjects all members of society to its power.

The democratic model, however, is the best alternative of those presently available. Its character is such that when a sufficient number of people are of another view, it can be used to disassemble the idea of centralistic power.

If we at this moment would change the character of the democratic, or any other system, to be in accordance with the spiritual laws, the consequence would be chaotic, since mankind isn't mature to implement something else. As long as people aren't in their own wills, they are not capable of implementing it.

The system's change into a more natural one happens gradually, when people one at a time take responsibility for themselves and their own original wills. When the number of free humans is sufficient, they can gradually change the system to be in accordance with the spiritual nature as they see fit. They will hardly rush the change to go faster that the maturing of mankind. Free humans can build the free world, and no blueprints are required for it.

The free world is based on a system, in which society isn't a forcing power, but the sum of people's own wills. It is not a sum as a compromise, but the sum that is born out of that every free will is fulfilled precisely as it is supposed to be fulfilled.

When own wills are fulfilled, their sum is equal to the overall thought, which the beings have created on the spiritual side. Own wills aren't any random matter, but they are parts of the entirety, in which the beings have unanimity and a mutual strive.

The condition of help in relation to the individual

In the so called civilized world, natural help isn't available for the children in any other sense than food and housing, and matters concerning those. Regarding thoughts, the child doesn't get help to naturally grow into being himself. His own will and the development to be himself is neglected. He is surrounded by a thought-world that is the tool of outer power to subdue the own will.

This subduing of the own will happens mostly by that the child from his environment copies a thought model that doesn't contain any knowledge which recognizes Self and the child's original own will. It contains only the mold of the existing society, into which the child is guided.

The own self and the own will are left without any attention and therefore the child's connection to Self isn't preserved, and the own will never develops as it should develop. The child submits to the world's thought and forgets his own, due to a practical must.

When the child grows towards adulthood, his connection to his own self is preserved for quite a long time. He doesn't easily experience a great conflict with the teaching of the world's thought, since the fulfilling of his own will isn't very necessary at that point, and he experiences to be able to postpone matters regarding it without problems.

When he continues to grow and one day is at the point, where he really should begin to fulfill his own original will, he can no longer remember it since his life is a long chain of submission and forgetting. For some the connection is strongly preserved for a long time, for some it disappears completely and they have therefore been fully transformed into being the world's thought's persons.

A person who still remembers himself is by nature in the thought of helping, regarding both the helping of others as well as getting help. For him the world's power structures, which displace the help he needs and would want to provide, are confusing. He is in a situation where he hasn't grown up to be his own person due to the lack of true help, and he lacks the sufficient knowledge and consciousness.

He has one foot in the own will's world, and one foot in the world he lives in. He experiences this division as very confusing and he might have difficulties to function in accordance with the world's thought, even if he tries. It can make him socially clumsy, since he can't reach the rhythm of the world's thought for the simple reason that he won't learn how to lie.

Some learn to live in that divided condition, and even to function smoothly in the world's thought without losing the connection to themselves and their own wills. However, this connection remains weak even at best. The person feels it and learns possibly even to listen to his own inside to some extent.

Many creative persons have preserved this kind of intermediate form between a true person and an upbrought person. That condition has also torn apart many creative persons. The biggest problem in that condition is that the person lacks knowledge and guidance to find the own self, which would lead to harmony.

Those who have forgotten themselves are balanced, since they have no conflict on the inside. Those who still remember themselves are more or less in pain, due to the conflict they have on the inside. They can weakly remember the own will and still experience a relation to Self. The memory is weak and the connection is weak. They mainly remember that there is something on the inside, but they don't have an answer to what it is.

In addition to this conflict formed by two worlds these persons experience disappointment, or the feeling of having been betrayed, since they weren't provided the help that they needed in childhood, and that they in accordance with the law of nature should have gotten. This disappointment can be a very strong feeling and it can tie up or paralyze the person very strongly.

The feeling of having been betrayed, or abandoned, is especially strong because the betrayal is true. It is not a feeling produced by a wrongly understood situation, but a well founded truth.

The free own will created by Self is created with the laws of nature as base, according to which the child should be helped to grow up to be himself and his natural freedom is recognized. In a situation where this is neglected and the child doesn't get any help in accordance with the natural system, but is instead directed into the lie of hierarchical power, the child will one day notice that he is in a trap, and therefore he will feel accordingly.

This noticing isn't a sudden notice of it, but a slowly evolving detection of the situation and it usually happens approximately in puberty. Many give up their own wills rather quietly. Some fight, without really knowing why. Regardless of how each person reacts to it, for those who don't forget themselves the disappointment remains in the mind.

If these pains are of visible harm for the human, the existing society offers adapting to the world's thought as the solution. It is the only help that is wanted to provide, since society in the present world doesn't experience anything else as real, and it isn't even interested of supporting anything else but the adapting of people to the existing ideas of good and functional members of society. In practice it means a human that has been subjected to an outer thought, in other words tempting into a lie and the forgetting of the truth.

For some the connection to Self is so weak that they willingly let go of it and adapt, since they experience it to be the easier alternative.

Some simply can't give up their connection to Self, since the connection is so strong that the persons experience it to be more important than a life in accordance with the world's thought.

Some of those persons can't manage to live because of the pain caused by the conflict, and instead they strive towards drugs, which they use to relieve their pain. Some are regardless of their pain capable of performing life, and their lives might contain something good which they deliver to mankind. In this context good means something that grows the freedom of the individuals, like art of high quality or something similar.

These persons are as a rule seekers to their nature. As a matter of fact, they are searching for a connection to themselves, whether they know it or not. They can be particularly prone of sensing things that are thought to be supernatural. They might create art, inventions and be pioneers. The only thing they won't do, is submitting to the world's thought.

Getting help is an advantage, but not a right

The goal of getting help must be the improvement of the own will's condition.

It is not a right to be helped, it is the helpers voluntary effort for one in need of help in some situation. No one can be obliged to help.

A correctly implemented providing of help serves everyone's interest, which is the growth of the overall freedom of the combined own wills.

The duty of the helped is to do his best, so that the effort of the helping could give the straightest possible route to the improvement of the own will's condition.

Seeking

Responsibility for the knowledge

The individual's responsibility for the knowledge is unconditional. That responsibility can't be pushed over to someone else.

When the person hears or reads something about something, the
responsibility for understanding the knowledge and the possible
revealing of a lie is the individual's own. He can't withdraw from
that responsibility for instance by blaming someone else for how
it influenced his thinking, actions and so on.

When the person receives knowledge, regardless of what it is, he
mustn't use it before he has understood its content, seen with his
own eyes what it is, and has had the clearest possible insight
about it.

Using knowledge before it is understood is comparable to that
one acquires and uses machines, without knowing what they are
and how to use them.

Research

The present science is in the name of objectivity using methods
that are to research the human inside from the outside.

It leads to the gathering of thought structures and logic in
accordance with those.

The weakness with that kind of inner research is that the researcher doesn't research his own inside, in which case he will never really have an insight of the essence of the inside, and he will never find the actual facts where those facts are. Then the reasons and sources aren't researched, but only the consequences. It is limited to be, even at best, observation of matters on the thought level.

With the help of those thought structures they are ready to monopolize all research and especially the counseling, which is called treatment.

Those who monopolize might not think that they are protecting their power, but believe the research to be free. As a matter of fact, it is not.

It has been limited inside the boundaries of the viewpoint they represent, and the fundamental thought of the viewpoint they represent is based on the viewpoint of hierarchical power, the needs it has defined and its concept of reality.

Moreover, the yearning for power is seen in that they see their viewpoint to be the highest power and truth of all research and knowledge. Their perception has to get to define even such knowledge they don't understand.

Even the treatment is a strive to power, in other words to get the patient to solve matters in the desired way and to recover in accordance with the view of life they represent, and which is based on forgetting oneself.

Since no counseling can help one to get where the viewpoint of that counseling is not, the help that the so called treatment offers doesn't lead in any other direction but the adapting to the offered view of life.

These views aren't based on the inner reality and the insight of it, they are based on thought models that have been built by using imagination.

The result of that treatment is the forgetting of Self and the adapting to the world's thought. If the treatment is successful, the person calms down, since the inner conflict decreases. The person is assumed to have recovered his health, since he has calmed down and begins to function in accordance with the behavior that is defined as normal.

In reality they don't see the inside of the person. They don't understand that the adapting didn't solve anything else but the externally visible restlessness. It didn't solve the real problem.

The real problem remains on the person's inside and it can rise up again if the person, against the adapting doctrine, begins to yearn for inner clarity and a connection to himself.

If the adapting doctrine doesn't work and the person doesn't calm down, he is seen to be in need of medication. The medication helps one to forget oneself and the result of it is often that the person calms down. When it isn't, the medication is for life and the person is seen to be incurably ill.

Real inner research is to go into the inner reality, opening it and seeing the truth. It is completely objective when the quality of the discoveries is sufficiently true, and not the products of imagination. For them not to be products of imagination, the person has to get very deep and reach full clarity first-handedly.

To reach a deep of research-level takes decades, and it is not reached by reading books and thinking. Only those whose original will is just that reaches it, for others it would be a stray path.

Other people can't find products of imagination inside them, but a correctly described inner reality they will find, if they haven't lost their connection to it. If the connection is lost, the person isn't capable of using the instructions usefully. By thinking it will never be found.

To solve problems is that the person himself studies his inner side, using guiding as help, which will ease the finding of the truth from the inside. Guiding doesn't ask one to believe, guiding helps one to find, to get insight. If the result is belief, it is not the solution to the problem.

The goal, when understanding oneself and looking for insight, can't be the learning of thought models. When those are understood, one only understands the consistency and images of those thought models.

It is copying of thought models, not understanding of the truth, and not insight of oneself or anything else.

For inner insight one needs guiding that is a sufficiently deep view of how the inside functions. Then one can with its help find what is sought for, in other words Self and the own real will, which is born from Self.

This way the person is freed from the inside, and he will find all the answers he has ever wanted to find in the matter.

Defending the truth

People have a tendency to create some idea and hold it for a truth. They defend that idea, since they want it to be true, and they want to believe they have already found the truth about that matter. If it were true, it wouldn't need to be defended. What is true is it without defending.

In this kind of defending, the event of defending itself is the person's inner rejection of the observation of the thought. If the person has reached a sufficient truth in the matter, it is completely clear to him all the time, and it won't change to anything else, even if it is questioned a thousand times.

Even a reached sufficient view can be clouded by someone with some knowledge, through which the person yet can't see the lie. Those are claims, whose strive is to distort the observation of the matter.

The distortion of the observation of the matter is done for instance with comparisons that are wrongly based, or with untruthful claims that feel believable. Depending on the level and clarity of the person's consciousness, he either sees or doesn't see through the lie. When a sufficient amount of time is used to observe the matter, it is possible to reveal the lie.

The most essential thing is inner honesty, in other words not to fight the new discovery if it is true. One must observe the matter peacefully until it is clear, to see if the offered knowledge was true or not. This way the observer becomes a winner in any case. The own view strengthens and the ability to observe matters grows.

The function of insight

An insight that opens up the consciousness functions so that the person for a very short while experiences a moment where the picture is clear. Directly afterwards the view, which the insight opened, closes leaving some improvement to ones understanding, but the enlightened state of that moment is not permanent, since the person isn't ready to confront it. Therefore he doesn't reach it, even if it for a short while is opened up.

One consequence of the opening and closing can be pain, like headache, stomach ache or a runny nose. These are examples of the body's reaction to that the person's consciousness of the obstacles grows to new areas. As fresh, that is just when they have come into mind, the obstacles are as strongest and therefore they can sometimes be even hard.

There is not at all always pain related to insight. Pain comes in those cases, where the insight at the same time frees one to notice obstacles in such a way, that they come within the area of the consciousness. It is common that greater and sudden growths of consciousness function like this.

This could be considered to be a bad thing, if the matter is observed from the viewpoint that the goal is a pleasant state. If the goal is a journey towards the truth, it is a good thing.

As a consequence of this kind of sudden opening the level of the person's problems grows, and when he has confronted them, he makes progress. Without it, he wouldn't make any progress at all. Without any earlier progress he wouldn't be in a condition, where it into the consciousness come problems, which weren't there earlier.

This means that after the short moment of opening, all that which prevents him from seeing, closes the opened view. The situation has, compared to the moment before, improved to the extent it has improved.

On the new area that was reached this way comes smaller insights, which free the person of the obstacles that prevented him from seeing the level that was closed. In these insights, the person experiences a feeling of liberation, since it is the freeing from lies.

The major part of the insights are related to clearing the confusion that already is in the consciousness, and where the person is successful in revealing the lies and obtaining the truth.

When it comes to an insight that is related to the growth of consciousness, one might imagine to have reached all that which for a brief moment flashed by as a lightning fast insight.

In fact, the person didn't reach it and therefore he isn't capable of explaining it in any way, besides if he, with the help of his imagination, invents descriptions that are based on imagination. They are not based on that flashing moment, since he simply isn't capable to reach the viewpoint of that flash.

Someone might be delighted to explain the viewpoint, which he experienced to be mighty. Then he is fascinated by the thought that he saw something great. When this feeling is strong, it can lead the human astray in a way where he rather imagines to have reached, than focuses on the confrontation of matters, so that he really could reach the viewpoint in question.

The opposite might also happen. The person might experience an insight that opens wide views, and when he notices that it closes up, he gets depressed and experiences that he will never reach it.

The truth is, however, that everyone who honestly seeks, and makes the sufficient effort to find, will find what he is looking for. The journey might be long and difficult, but the result is guaranteed if one doesn't run out of time. If one runs out of time, the force of the will moves to the next life, and the journey continues.

The target of observation

The target of observation is primarily the inner reality, since only that way the own viewpoint can be moved closer to Self. Observation of the environment is for the major part important after that, since the higher and clearer the viewpoint from which one observes is, the better prerequisites it gives to understand the environment.

Observation of the environment is primary in a case, where the person is suppressed by many lies in such way that he isn't able to focus on the observation of the inner world. Then he must first manage to reveal the lies that cause the problem, so that their force is canceled. Overcoming them requires an understanding that happens in a viewpoint that is on a sufficient level, in which case they are revealed and their force disappears.

The purer the person can observe the world remaining in the viewpoint of his own real person, the better he understands the nature of the world. His possibility of seeing the world's lie improves when the viewpoint approaches Self.

When the person begins to observe his inner world, and also the outer world, trying to understand them better, he is able to understand them on some level. The level rises when the observation is continued and gradually he approaches the level that is his basic level, meaning the starting level, seen from the viewpoint of the fulfilling of his own will.

Only from his starting level can he fully begin to fulfill his own real will. Before that the seeking for the starting level is urgent and it should be a very central matter. Other doings shouldn't be rushed at this point, and they shouldn't be valued to be more important than the necessary need. From that on the raising of the level normalizes and it is raised in accordance to the need gradually.

The progress of the confrontation

When unconscious areas are looked into, something gradually begins to come into mind, in other words, as a distance to the person it rises to the level "forget" on the distance table.

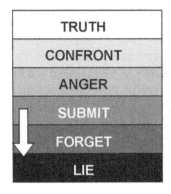 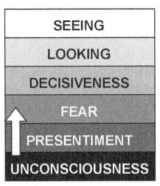

TRUTH	SEEING
CONFRONT	LOOKING
ANGER	DECISIVENESS
SUBMIT	FEAR
FORGET	PRESENTIMENT
LIE	UNCONSCIOUSNESS

Corresponding to the level of forgetting is the rising into mind, which in this pair of pictures is on the right side as "presentiment". Then a weak presentiment of the matter begins to come into mind.

When the matter rises more into the mind, it moves to the level "fear", which corresponds to submission. The fear is caused by many things.

A part of it is the fear of the revealing of the truth. Then something that oneself has hidden comes into mind. It is the reason to that he once lowered his consciousness.

The other part is related to the thought models, on top of which the person's life is. The growth of truth reveals the lies and therefore it changes the person's life, and sometimes the changes might be very big.

In any case, while the person progresses towards his own real selfhood, the thoughts that control his life crumble piece by piece. They are supposed to crumble.

If we are to express it strongly, we could say that the artificial person has to die. It means that the person built on top of the world's thought seizes to exist, when the person reaches his own self sufficiently.

If the person quickly would really confront the thought models, on top of which his life is built, he might very well leave everything right there, and begin building new out of nothing. More usual is that the person gradually changes his life, as his understanding of matters change, in other words as he changes his thought models.

There is a diversity of fears and they might contain pain. Fear in this context is a state, where the person is aware of his existing state and how the matters that are rising to be visible affect it, and that makes him uncertain. He knows that he as a consequence of it must abandon many things, which he in that moment still considers to be important to him.

Many give up directly when fear is knocking on the door, and withdraw. They don't want to confront painful matters, but want to find painless states. They don't know that confrontation leads to freedom, and that withdrawal leads to an ever decreasing consciousness and the captivity of one's own fears.

The influence of fear isn't present only when the person experiences conscious fear. He might know that certain areas contain unpleasant things, and he solves it by not looking on that area. In that case the reason is also fear, even if the feeling of fear doesn't appear.

When he approaches the maturity to confront the matter, he grows his strength by getting angry, which in this context also is to create decisiveness, and when the strength is sufficient, he goes through the wall of fear.

Confrontation is resolute observation of the matter, without prejudices, without distortion or avoiding anything. It is to look directly towards the matter.

When he sees completely clearly, he has reached the level of truth in the matter that he was supposed to reach. One must be thorough and confront all the way to the end, for the matter in question to have been seen fully and unconditionally.

Abandoning

Abandoning

Abandoning is to let go of a thought.

Lies stay in the life of the human, since he holds on to them himself.

The truth doesn't have to be held on to, it never disappears.

Abandoning is a prerequisite to be free from lies. If the person holds on to lies, he can't find the truth, since he himself close his way to the truth.

Abandoning is to let go, which simplest form is to cease to let some thought influence one's actions. When the person uses some thought, he strengthens it. When he stops using it, he weakens it.

Abandoning is completely safe. The person can abandon everything, even that which is true. That which is lie, won't come back again, when the abandoning has been performed to its full. That which is true, won't ever disappear, no matter how much one would abandon it and how many times. It is always there and returns to one's sight again and again.

The abandoning isn't completed at once. When the person abandons some thought, he lets go of it on the level he is able to. It is not removed completely, but it gets weaker. When the abandoning is performed several times, it weakens more. At some point, when the person has succeeded in revealing its lie, it disappears permanently.

By abandoning it is weakened and the revealing of the lie gets easier.

While the lies disappear, the truth will rise up from underneath them since it has never been lost, it has only been hidden behind the lies.

The effect of abandoning

Any binding to something is formed out of the thought to maintain that binding. The difference between the truth and the lie is that the truth doesn't have to be tied with a thought. It is there, since it belongs there, and the lie must be tied with a thought, since otherwise it won't stay there.

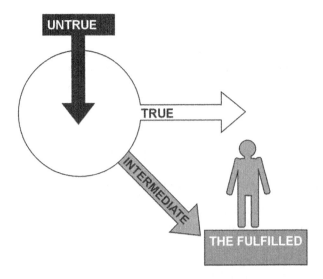

In the picture the untrue is a force that influences the person's movement, and that which is true is distorted by it. Then the person's movement is an intermediate form between the truth and the lie. In that case the fulfilled isn't what his will was.

When the person holds on to a lie, he holds on to it because he thinks it is true. Therefore he doesn't notice that it is a lie, and he might experience the holding on to it as very important. Even so important, that he believes his life to be dependant of it.

He sees that the result of his life is something else than he wants, but he doesn't understand the reason to it. He might strive to convince himself, that his life is great and that it is what he wants, but on the inside he knows that it is not.

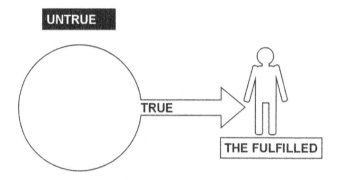

In this picture the person has abandoned the untrue, in other words the maintaining of the lie, and therefore it no longer has an influence. Then the only influencing factor is the truth about the own will, and it is the only thing that is fulfilled.

This change is what occurs when the person abandons lies.

One must notice, that any thought structure that isn't completely true is a lie, since even the part in it that would be true is distorted by the lie. Therefore one can't think that it is after all a little true. If it is not completely true, then it is a lie and must be abandoned.

The difficulty of abandoning

The further away the person is from himself, the more materialistic he experiences life and gets his satisfaction from material values. Then the relation to Self is very distant. Practically seen the person has lost his connection to his own thought and it is very difficult for him to notice, that the life he lies to himself to be a good life, in fact is something that he originally didn't even want.

A clear obstacle for the abandoning is that the human is afraid to lose something when abandoning. He believes that he will lose something he already has. He doesn't in fact have anything, but he holds on to something and is its prisoner. One could say that the lie has the human on the hook. Since the purpose of the lie is to keep the person under the power of someone else's thought, the person really is a prisoner of the lie.

A lie that keeps one as its prisoner also contains the claims with which it explains its importance. If the lie isn't offered in such a form that the person is made to believe in its importance, the person will never take it. Therefore he believes it to be important and necessary to keep.

The values that the lie offers are a strong binding factor, since the person's set of values is very central in the defining of what is important and what is not. These values are to their nature such that they look beautiful and good, but are in fact not.

Revealing the lies of the values can be very difficult, since the person is tied to them in many ways. They have bindings to the person's whole life, and furthermore, he shares those values with possibly many other humans. Revealing the lies of the values then also weakens the person's ties to the environment, and he might experience to lose important human relations.

Regardless of how wide the human relations are, if they are based on wrong values, they are not true, and the understanding of those human relations isn't true. Those human relations tie up the person, and are in no case good for him.

He might experience fear of being left alone, if he would abandon the thoughts that tie him to a group. Because of this he might be ready to lie to himself even consciously and strive to strengthen the tie he discovered to be untrue, by strengthening the lie to himself. In that case he strives to defend the thought strongly, to strengthen the tie of the lie. He might even succeed in quieting the voice of the truth inside him, but the price for it is the weakening of the connection to the own self, or even its disappearance.

Another phenomenon of the same matter is a human who is withdrawn. He has isolated himself from others by withdrawing into his own world. He protects his world by weakening the contact to other people. He builds his own set of values and lives with it in his own world.

The problem of abandoning is for him very much that he is afraid of losing the defense, which he with a lot of effort has built, and his separate world, which he experiences to be safe. Since he once experienced it to be the only way to secure himself, he is afraid of its opening up, and experiences it as a threat.

It is, however, unnecessary for him to be afraid of losing that structure more than losing any other lies. When the person abandons lies, he grows stronger, since the amount of truth grows. When abandoning, the truth is never at risk, since it doesn't disappear.

The fear of losing something is a strong obstacle to the ability to abandon. The person might experience to lose everything. He is not much mistaken, since when abandoning everything, he will lose all the old relations to persons as well as things. Instead a new relation to each thing and person arises. This new relation is more true than the earlier one.

The building materials of life

Thought model

People create a life that builds on the thought models they use, and which define their ideas of life.

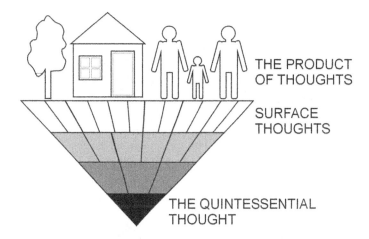

THE PRODUCT
OF THOUGHTS

SURFACE
THOUGHTS

THE QUINTESSENTIAL
THOUGHT

The thought models are built in layers, so that there is a quintessential idea of life and on top of it is built thoughts, which are closer to the surface and which define the details of life. The closer to the surface some idea is, the easier it is to change, but only on the terms of the deeper thoughts.

The original purpose has been that the quintessential though is the person's own thought. It is the own and self created will regarding life.

The own thought isn't a thought in the same sense as thoughts in general. It is not lie that is maintained by using imagination, but it is the basic idea of the own person and the own person's life.

The accuracy of the own will as the life controlling factor varies. Depending on the purpose, it can contain more or less accurate details. The own will in some cases is very precise in its definitions of the life course, and in others the definitions are wider. The precision depends on how significant it is for the fulfilling of the own will.

Changing of the thought model

The quintessential thought can be very difficult to question. If the quintessential thought is changed, or a part of it is removed, then everything built on top of it disappears at the same time. The only quintessential thought that can't be removed is the thought of the own will, which is as permanent as the truth.

The own thought can be covered with lies and the truth can be covered with lies. They fade from view, but they don't disappear.

Lies are a product of imagination. They are thoughts that are maintained as long as they are maintained. They disappear when they are revealed to the one who maintains them, in other words the person himself.

The quintessential thought is very deep in the unconsciousness. The route to it goes through the thoughts that are built on top of it. The knowledge of it and its nature isn't enough to disassemble it. The person needs to himself in his mind see the quintessential thought that, when the world's thought is in question, is a quintessential lie.

The changes in the quintessential thought can be quite slow and even difficult since the full confrontation of them, in other words the seeing of them, is very demanding and the thought model also contains a protection, so that the different parts support each other and require the maintaining of each other.

Performing changes can cause confusion, since the questioning and the changing of some parts put the other parts in a conflict in relation to the parts that are the subject of the change.

The changes might also include pain. The pain is born out of the difference between the own believed state and believed wanted state. For example, the growth of the awareness of the distance between the own will and the present state causes pain to the extent that distance is acknowledged.

If the thought model the person maintains is shaken for some reason, he might be put in an imbalanced state. This can be born out of some strong factor that questions the image of life the person maintains. It might as well be born out of the person's own insight regarding his life.

A strong factor could be some great change in life, especially if it is very sudden.

The imbalance is born out of the conflicts which occur in the thought models, and which confuse the person's mind.

The conflict is born either of that the person in his set of ideas has learned thoughts, which are in conflict with each other, or that the person is conscious, or becomes conscious, of his own will and experiences the conflict between the learned and the own thought.

The conflict exists until some thought model becomes dominant. The confusion that is born out of the conflicts decreases as the different effects of the person's thought model become parallel.

When the parts of the person's set of ideas become parallel, the confusion decreases and it is easier for him to act, regardless of how true the new situation is.

The person might learn to accept as truths some ideas that are commonly accepted good ideas. They are the world's thought. This produces harmony, but it also prevents the rise of the person's own thought.

The person can solve the imbalance also by confronting his own will on a sufficient level. Then he strengthens the true independence and a permanent balance that isn't dependent of others or the world's thought.

In both cases the conflict of thoughts, which was the reason to the imbalance, disappears and is replaced by balance. The only solution that removes the problem is to approach the own will. The support sought from the world's thought doesn't remove the problem, it only covers the problem.

Thought models are built in such way, that each part supports the other and therefore the removal of individual areas doesn't work very well.

To approach his own will, the person has to widely confront his whole thought model, and then he is able to weaken it, so that the own thought can begin to rise more into the mind. In this context there is reason to remember, that real confrontation isn't thinking, but looking at matters without thinking.

Quite few observe the foundations of their lives in such a way, that they would question the goodness of the quintessential thought models they use. They are brought up into them and consider them to be self-evident truths.

They experience that those thought models are the truth about life and the purpose of life. Therefore they only ponder over the structures built on top of those thought models. They think and create new thoughts into the structures of the earlier thoughts and on their terms.

The world's thought at this moment is completely the game of hierarchical power, which hardly anyone questions. If one wants to question some quintessential thought model, he must go to its roots, anything less isn't enough.

The quintessential thought about life, which the person has inside him, controls his life completely. It is not a question of conscious thinking, but the concept of reality. It can be changed, but then one must rise above it. In any other case it is the dominant thought.

It can only be removed by revealing its lie, not by thinking, but with an inner insight of it. By thinking it can't be broken and removed. It can be weakened and it can be opposed by thinking, but it doesn't cease to influence.

The wrong life

Seen to the own thought, the life of the world's thought is a wrong life. The only right life is the life that is defined by the own will. Only the creation of it is the right life and an own life.

People commonly believe that the own life is the life they fulfill, but when life isn't controlled by the own real will, life isn't one's own. Some other thought is fulfilled in the person, and he himself is only a passenger in the life he is fulfilling.

The attraction of the wrong life

The more implementers some thought about life has, the more it attracts each and everyone, and the weaker one's own will is, the more it influences one.

The world's thought attracts one very easily, since it is an idea of life that the human is taught already as a child. There is no support for a life built on the own will, and its existence is not even recognized.

Since the dominant thought doesn't support a life of the own will, the life of the own will isn't as attractive, since being part of almost anything else is to live according to the world's thought.

When young people begin to choose their direction, they usually still have a connection to the own thought. They might be very aware of that the offered life doesn't correspond with the wanted life.

This consciousness of the own will can't rise up to be dominant, since the young one doesn't remember what it is. Therefore the own will's influence on life is slight at best.

There is so little space for the own will's world in the present world, that there are very few who are capable of it even to some degree, since that would require a very clear idea and a deep insight of what the own will and Self are.

Happiness

Happiness is nearness to Self and the own will. It is movement towards the fulfilling of the own purpose. It is approaching of the truth and the growth of inner clearness.

The feeling of happiness is very commonly sought in the feeling of comfort, which is searched for in a painless state.

It is searched for by the means of inner dishonesty, so that one doesn't look at matters as they are and is in that way able to convince oneself that one lives in the truth.

Happiness is very much sought for in entertainment and pleasures, which are used as attention catchers to cover the inner pain and emptiness.

Happiness is tried to be created with pictures, which in fact is the harmony of images created on the level of imagination, not inner reality.

Happiness isn't born out of painlessness, easiness or thought-images, but it is born out of approaching the truth.

Its approaching isn't always painless or easy, but it brings inner balance and makes it grow. It strengthens the consciousness of the own life purpose, and the fulfilling of that purpose brings the only satisfaction that is based on the truth.

The challenge of life

The easy life

It is common to man to look for simplicity and easiness to life in laziness. This can be seen in such a way, that the observation of life and all learning is experienced to be heavy, and relief is sought in not observing, or learning.

It is considerably much easier not learning to read, than learning to read. That is true, but life as a literate is easier than life as an illiterate.

Taking responsibility for the observing of matters all the way to the point where one understands is heavier than not to observe, but correspondingly living in inability is heavier than living in ability.

So, easiness to life is often sought in laziness, which in fact doesn't make life easier, but it makes it heavier. The human hides this laziness from himself by thinking that he isn't lazy, he just doesn't want to.

Very usually people's attitude towards learning and doing is that they think isn't this enough already, which is a clear sign of laziness. As if there would exist some instance that rewards one, when one has made some efforts. Life doesn't reward anything but the fully learned and the fully completed. Life doesn't reward incompleteness.

The fact is that if the person doesn't study anything, or does it poorly, then he is lazy.

This kind of laziness has many bad consequences. The most significant consequence is, however, the ignorance and inability to understand the own life, the world and the relations between them.

The understanding of the own life requires the raising of the own will and the revealing of the errors in the world's thought. That can't be reached by being, that can be reached by concentrating on the matter and working for it until it is so clear to oneself, that the person reaches himself. Without this the person neglects the purpose of his life.

The ignorant is easy to lead astray and the reason to it is in the person's own choices, not in anything else from his viewpoint seen.

Alternatively we could think, that the persons who lead astray are guilty, but it wouldn't be possible if the person would take responsibility for himself.

Laziness in relation to the own original will is as a distance on the level of forgetting. The person wants to forget, or he doesn't have the energy to remember.

Matters outside of the own will don't fall on him, so he has no reason to study them.

The world's thought offers things, which in no way concerns the own will, and regarding them the person doesn't experience any interest, besides in the case where he lies to himself that he wants those things.

People mostly get a though-image of will from the thought-images offered by the world's thought. They define their will based on the thought-images learnt from the world's thought. The own original will is in a subjected state, and raising it to be dominant is difficult under the present circumstances of the world.

The negligence to study the own person is a combination of fear and laziness. Laziness is drowsiness, in other words as a distance on the level of forgetting. Fear as a distance is on the level of submission.

The person is afraid to study the own person and he would like to solve the problem by looking elsewhere. However, the person can't get rid of himself by looking elsewhere, he has to live with his own person for the rest of his life.

The negligence of the observation of life and learning also leads to that finding the own real selfhood isn't possible, and furthermore, the person is at the mercy of others due to his own ignorance. He is easier to control if he isn't his own real self and doesn't understand life.

People give away their responsibility for themselves to others very willingly, since they believe it makes it easier to themselves. That also is the ideal of the power system, since power doesn't exist, if it is not given. We might as well say that power is taken by subjecting, but the subjecting is possible only when the person himself accepts it.

This giving away of the responsibility leads only to that the person's life to that part is limited to others decisions.

In fact, others can't take responsibility for the person, since the person's only responsibility, in other words the fulfilling of the own purpose, requires that he seeks, finds and fulfills it himself.

Neither will they take the responsibility for the consequences that the person has to live with, no matter if he has influenced them himself or not.

At the feet of power

There are many who desire power over others. The user of power can be a person, or many persons, in the circle of acquaintances of the human. The same strive to power exists stepwise all the way to the leaders of the state. States on the other hand strive to use power in relation the each other.

The state, and the power system of its parts, suppresses the individual's freedom, and it demands that the individual abandons his own freedom. Abandoning the natural freedom is in this respect quite inevitable. The refusal of it is usually not possible, since it would lead to an even worse condition.

The demands of many others who desire power can on the other hand mostly be refused. Sometimes it goes through a conflict, if the one who desires power strives to subject, and doesn't give up immediately.

Rulers, and those who consider themselves to be rulers, are always satisfied when people themselves don't want to take responsibility for themselves. The only responsibilities they want people to take are the responsibilities that the rulers have chosen.

To be able to fully live a life in accordance to the own will, the person has to be aware of the existence of humans in his environment who suppress his own thought, and learn to identify the suppression.

The suppression is best repelled by raising the own consciousness above those lies in such way, that one doesn't any longer have their equivalent, in other words unanimity with them, in the own mind. Then one can observe the lie in the other person's mind, but it no longer has any effect on the own mind.

Many attempts to suppress can be such, that it is difficult to find the lie in them, in other words to recognize the lie, but one can clearly feel their suppressing effect. In that case a way to defend oneself is simply by not agreeing to join the proposed way of thinking, but to observe it in one's own peace until one understands what is lie in it. When the lie is revealed, the pressure of that thought ceases.

Even if one doesn't manage to see what the lie is in such where one can clearly feel the attempt to suppress and the attempt to power, it is good to refuse it.

The offered thoughts can be like weapons that are used in an attempt to defeat the person, and get him to act in accordance to someone else's desire.

It is always an attempt to power when the offered thought weakens the development of the person's own free will and the growth of inner clarity.

The pressure that is used to get the person to confront his own person, and to get him to take responsibility for his own self, can sometimes feel like that the freedom of the person's conscious will is weakened.

The difference is that it is possible for the person to recognize, with the help of his inner honesty, the claimed knowledge as true, and moreover, he can discover that the pressure doesn't stop the rising of the own will, but helps it to be freed.

Helping pressure is always such that it disappears, when the person's own will honestly appears. The final result must be that the person's own will is more functional than before.

The own will's relation to the whole life

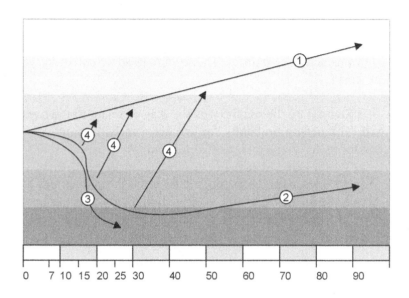

The numbers at the bottom of the diagram are the person's different ages, and the arrows illustrate the person's movement in time compared to the state of their own wills during the whole life.

The white at the top illustrates the fulfilled own will, which is equal to the growth of consciousness in relation to the goal. The darker gray at the bottom illustrates the lowering of the consciousness all the way to that the connection to the own will disappears.

The diagram isn't precise in such way, that the persons' ages or paths of motion are exactly like that. There are countless possibilities, so the diagram is describing, not absolute.

Case 1 moves steadily all the way from birth to the fulfilling of his life's purpose. This doesn't occur in the present world.

Case 2 bows under the power of the world's thought, but preserves a quite good connection to himself. He manages in some degree to do something in the direction of his own will, but it is laborious and even painful. This occurs to some extent in the present world.

Case 3 is favored by the majority as the way to relate to the own real will. The person gradually forgets his own will completely, and transforms fully into an artificial person.

The arrowed lines with the number 4 describe the movement of case 2 from the influence of the world's thought towards the own thought. The younger he is when he begins, the faster it is done, since the distance to the own thought is shorter.

Case 3 loses the connection at the age of 20-30 years, and he no longer has any connection to himself, so it is very unlikely that he would get interested enough to do something about it. It is possible, but very unlikely.

We must notice, that there are a lot of differences between the possible paths of motion of the individuals.

The significance of the base of life

Life can't be better than the base that is built.

Life is built on a base that is on some level, and that functions as the basic thought of the created life.

The basic thought must be of sufficient quality and level for the intended life.

The only real option as the base of life is the person's own original will regarding his life. This requires the growth of consciousness in such a way, that the person sufficiently clearly manages to reach himself.

The human of the present world is to the degree unaware of his inner selfhood, that he can't understand it to be the quintessential base that life is built upon. Therefore this base is in a bad shape and the only thing that usually is strived to do regarding it, is not to look at it, in other words it is tried to suppress into oblivion. This is based on the imagining that it won't disturb life, if it isn't on the surface and visible.

Forgetting doesn't solve the problem, it only extinguishes the person's connection to himself and narrows his consciousness. It brings the person closer to the world's thought and distances him from the own thought.

The outer world is internally in such a condition, that the experience of Self is nonexistent. It is not spoken of, and its existence is strived to quiet down by raising up the values of the outer world and the materialistic world view to the position of the real base for life.

For some the consciousness is preserved even strong. For them it might cause serious problems, since the conflict with the present concepts of reality is strong. This condition the world sees adversely and assumes that the persons with visible problems are somehow useless.

This distorted set of values leads to the emphasis of the exterior and hiding of the inner pains. Many strive to protect their reputation to any price by hiding the inner pain and the possible foolish actions caused by it.

The great task of entertainment is to help people to shift the focus from the awareness of the inner condition. People party and act funny and happy to the best of their ability, but on the inside there is pain to the extent the person still is conscious of himself. Those who have lost their connection don't feel any pain because of it, but usually even they can experience the inner emptiness, the meaninglessness.

Relaxation that is produced by entertainment is good, when it is used appropriately, but if it is used to fill out life, it is only a drug that is used to cover the inner condition, that one doesn't want to take responsibility for.

Entertainment is in the present world a considerable tool to make the controlling of people easier.

To free the world

To free the mankind

The nature of mankind is our own creation. It is born of our mutual communication.

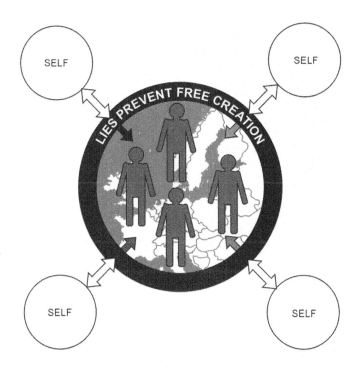

At the present state, those who create mankind aren't in control over the creation. This means that the own will's of the beings aren't the instance that controls the creation. So many lies have come into the creation, that those lies control the lives instead of each and everyone himself.

As an entirety mankind is therefore not free. Some are certainly in control and everyone takes part in the hierarchical power system in one way or another. In this respect the creation is still our own. What isn't fulfilled is the original and pure free will. We have created a world that no one actually wants, but we all maintain it together.

The problem can be solved by creating and spreading guiding among mankind, with help of which we can begin to disassemble the lie. The purpose of Alkuajatus is to break through the existing world's thought and initiate the disassembling of it.

To the actual clearing it isn't enough that guiding exists on paper and that there are a few persons who are capable of guiding. To disassemble the lies, each and everyone must disassemble them for himself, since what is fulfilled as the mankind, is all our relations to our own wills.

As long as our relation to our own wills is weak, the sum of our fulfilled wills is filled with lies.

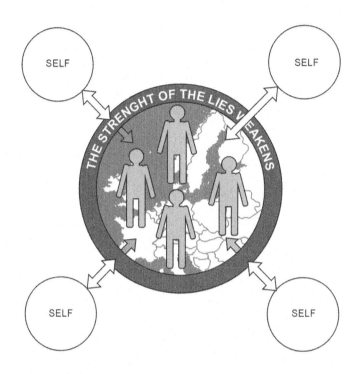

As the lies are disassembled on an individual level, the power of the lies decreases in each and everyone himself, as well as in the whole.

Every insight done by the individual is a piece of that disassembling of the lie. Every lie has to be disassembled, it can't be avoided. Every time someone has an insight and frees the truth, the world changes exactly as much as he reduced the lie in the world.

With every insight everyone is bringing light to the world, and is changing it towards the world that we really want. It is the only way to bring the truth to the world. There are no other ways.

Every insight that frees the person from the influence of lies, frees the world from the influence of lies, since the person is a part of the world.

Partly the light is born out of that the persons reduce the existing lie, and partly because they give space to the own free wills of the coming generations. Every ray of light is repeated in the children who are given a better world as the base of their lives.

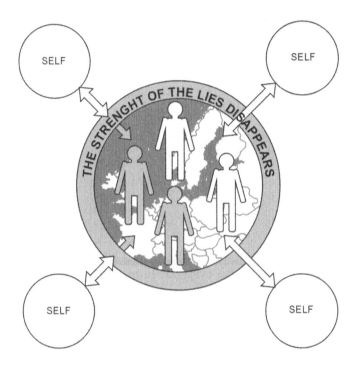

The lie of the world's thought will inevitably be defeated, if people want that. Defeating it doesn't happen with a revolution, or political work. It happens by disassembling the lies, since the free world can't be created if there are no persons, who are free from lies.

The freer of lies the world is in average, the less the lie influences the world. When the lie decreases, its disassembling accelerates and its strength disappears.

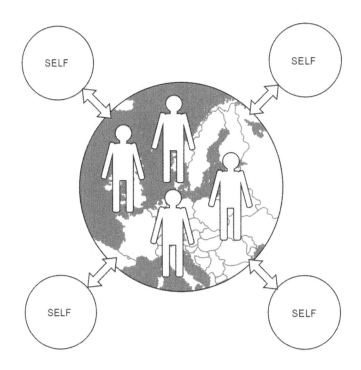

Free humans create a free world by their nature. It doesn't have to be taught to them, and we don't have to create instructions to them. They know what they are doing, since it is the purpose of their own original wills.

The road to that condition is long, and possibly stony, but it is the only alternative, since no other alternatives correspond to our own wills.

So let us stop lying to ourselves.

Extended Table of Contents

Alkuajatus study circles

In the study circles one can go into subjects offered by Alkuajatus in detail. The reading of the book helps one to understand the subjects in the study circles, and the study circles help one to understand the book.

Study circles are also available online.

Read more on the home page:

www.alkuajatus.org

9 789522 865304